PIGS IN THE PARLOR
STUDY GUIDE

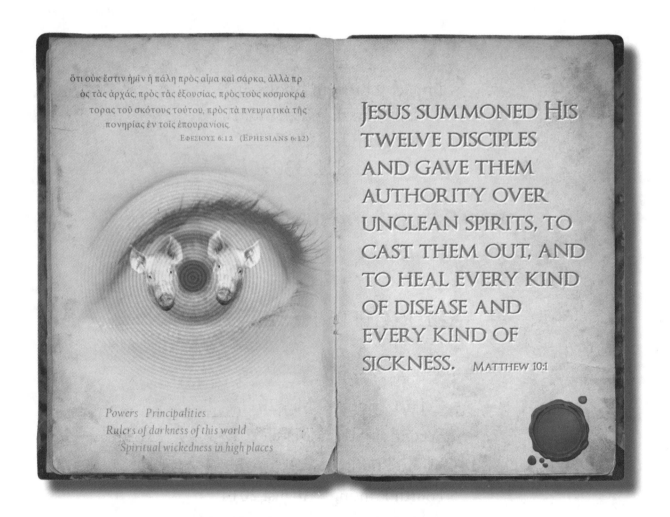

ὅτι οὐκ ἔστιν ἡμῖν ἡ πάλη πρὸς αἷμα καὶ σάρκα, ἀλλὰ πρ
ὸς τὰς ἀρχάς, πρὸς τὰς ἐξουσίας, πρὸς τοὺς κοσμοκρά
τορας τοῦ σκότους τούτου, πρὸς τὰ πνευματικὰ τῆς
πονηρίας ἐν τοῖς ἐπουρανίοις.
ΕΦΕΣΙΟΥΣ 6:12   (EPHESIANS 6:12)

Powers Principalities
Rulers of darkness of this world
Spiritual wickedness in high places

JESUS SUMMONED HIS TWELVE DISCIPLES AND GAVE THEM AUTHORITY OVER UNCLEAN SPIRITS, TO CAST THEM OUT, AND TO HEAL EVERY KIND OF DISEASE AND EVERY KIND OF SICKNESS.   MATTHEW 10:1

Based on the book by
Frank & Ida Mae Hammond

STUDY GUIDE: Pigs in the Parlor
ISBN 10: 0-89228-199-5
ISBN 13: 978-089228-199-2

Copyright © 2011
Impact Christian Books

Based on the book *Pigs in the Parlor* by Frank & Ida Mae Hammond
Written by S. Banks

Impact Christian Books, Inc.
332 Leffingwell Ave., Suite 101
Kirkwood, MO 63122
(314)-822-3309

www.impactchristianbooks.com

First Printing   May 2011
Second Printing   March 2012
Third Printing   March 2013
Fourth Printing   August 2014
Fourth Printing   September 2015

Printed in the United States of America

TABLE OF CONTENTS

SECTION IV: SETTING OTHERS FREE - THE DELIVERANCE MINISTRY

INTRODUCTION

This Study Guide has been designed with you in mind.

➤ If you are in search of deliverance for yourself or for someone you love, this companion book to *Pigs in the Parlor* has been designed as a tool to enable you to diagnose and effectively deal with your deliverance needs.

➤ This guide emphasizes the scriptural basis for the deliverance ministry, and has been designed as a Biblical resource to detail the extensive coverage of this topic in the Old and New Testaments.

➤ If you are feeling led to become involved in a deliverance ministry of your own, to help set captives free, this guide has an entire section on the methods and techniques, the pro's and con's of how to effectively minister deliverance.

Each chapter in *Pigs in the Parlor* has a corresponding chapter in this study guide. However, the order has been rearranged so that there are four areas of study:

I.   An Introduction to Deliverance

II. How Demons Manifest in our Daily Lives

III. The Process of Becoming and Staying Free

IV. Setting Others Free – The Deliverance Ministry

Because the order of the Study Guide does not always follow the order of Chapters in *Pigs in the Parlor*, there are really two ways to use this Study Guide.

1. *First*, you can read the book *Pigs in the Parlor* completely, and then use this Study Guide as a workbook to go through the material in the book again. As you work through each section, you will be able to focus on the four main objectives listed above: to introduce yourself to deliverance, to learn how demons manifest in our daily lives, to walk through the process of being liberated from demonic oppression, and finally, to learn how to set others free.

2. *Second*, you can, if you prefer, use this Study Guide concurrently as you are reading *Pigs in the Parlor*. In this case, you will find each chapter of *Pigs in the Parlor* listed in the Study Guide Table of Contents, and you can jump to the lesson that corresponds to the chapter you are on.

Either way will be effective in assisting you in your quest for knowledge of deliverance.

You will need your Bible at hand, as there are many powerful scriptures to examine. We have left space for answers to each question, but you should feel free to expand on your personal reflections in your own journal or notebook. This is especially true of Section II, which focuses on meeting your personal deliverance needs.

Our prayer is that with the book *Pigs in the Parlor*, and its companion Study Guide, you will be enabled to more fully appropriate the material Frank and Ida Mae Hammond presented, and to receive the help you are seeking.

Authored & Compiled by
Susan Banks and Stephen Banks
Impact Christian Books

Based on the book *Pigs in the Parlor*
by Frank & Ida Mae Hammond

Books, Booklets & Audio ~ Video
by Frank & Ida Mae Hammond

BOOKS

The Breaking of Curses

Comfort for the Wounded Spirit

Demons & Deliverance

A Manual for Children's Deliverance

Kingdom Living for the Family

Overcoming Rejection

Pigs in the Parlor

Saints at War

BOOKLETS

Confronting Familiar Spirits

Soul Ties

Repercussions from Sexual Sins

The Marriage Bed

Forgiving Others

Our Warfare

The Father's Blessing

God Warns America

The Perils of Passivity

Promoted by God

The Strongman of Unbelief

The Tales of Two Franks

Obstacles to Deliverance: *Why Deliverance Sometimes Fails*

DVDs

Breaking Demonic Soul Ties

The Schizophrenia Revelation

Binding the Strongman

Mind, Will & Emotions

Obstacles to Deliverance

Breaking Curses

The Wiles of the Devil

Deliverance from Self

Can a Christian Have a Demon?

Poltergeists: Demons in the Home

COMPACT DISCS

The Deliverance Series

Freedom from Bondage

The End-Time Series

Family in the Kingdom

Faith Series

Walk in the Spirit Series

Spiritual Meat Series

The Church Series

Message on Love

Recognizing God

www.impactchristianbooks.com

QUOTES ON DELIVERANCE & THE GIFTS OF THE SPIRIT

FROM THE EARLY CHURCH (100 – 400 A.D.)

COMPILED FROM A *LETTER TO DR. CONYERS MIDDLETON* (1749 A.D.)
PUBLISHED FROM: "THE LETTERS OF THE REV. JOHN WESLEY" VOL 2.
"GIFTS OF THE HOLY SPIRIT" JOHN WESLEY

The following quotes were cited in the above letters by John Wesley. These quotes were from the earliest church fathers that followed the apostles; from the mid-100's to the 4th century. They confirm that miraculous works, the casting out of demons, healing the sick, and the gifts of the Spirit were all in operation well after the close of the Book of Acts. In fact, they were commonplace!

For instance, according to WESLEY, during this period: "The raising of the dead was not for conversion of heathens but for the good of the church."

Following are a number of confirmations from early Church fathers that the Church in the 1st – 4th Centuries was actively casting out demons, healing the sick, and in general continuing the miraculous ministry of Jesus Christ according to John 14:12: *"Most assuredly, I say to you, he who believes in Me, the works that I do he will do also; and greater works than these he will do, because I go to My Father."*

1. JUSTIN MARTYR (MID 103–165 A.D., CHRISTIAN APOLOGIST AND SAINT)

"There are prophetic gifts among us even until now. You may see with this both men and women having gifts from the Spirit of God." He particularly insisted upon casting out devils as the gift that everyone might see with his own eyes.

2. IRANEUS (CIRCA 202 A.D., BISHOP OF LUGDUNUM IN GAUL)

"That all who were truly disciples of Jesus wrought miracles in His name: Some cast out devils, others had visions or knowledge of future events, others healed the sick." He went further to state that the "raising of the dead was often accomplished by great fasting and joint supplication of the church. Many speak in tongues."

3. THEOPHILUS (LATE 2ND CENTURY A.D., BISHOP OF ANTIOCH)

"Casting out devils is commonplace."

4. TERTULLIAN (END OF 2ND CENTURY A.D., EARLY CHRISTIAN AUTHOR & PRIEST)

He challenged the heathen magistrates to "call before their tribunals any person possessed with a devil." He went further to state that if a Christian could not get the evil spirit to show himself then the Christian was not a legitimate one.

5. MINUTIUS FELIX (3RD CENTURY A.D., CHRISTIAN APOLOGIST)

In a letter addressed to the heathen: "The greatest part of you know what confessions the demons make concerning themselves when we expel them out of the bodies of men."

6. ORIGEN (3RD CENTURY A.D., AFRICAN CHRISTIAN SCHOLAR & THEOLOGIAN)

He wrote that he saw "all the Spiritual gifts and healings manifested by common Christians."

7. CYPRIAN (3RD CENTURY A.D., BISHOP OF CARTHAGE)

"Even children are filled with the Holy Spirit [with speaking in tongues]" and he specifically mentions casting out devils and illnesses healed.

8. ARNOBIUS (CIRCA 303 A.D., CHRISTIAN APOLOGIST)

"Christ's name puts evil spirits to flight."

9. LACTANTIUS (4TH CENTURY A.D., CHRISTIAN AUTHOR AND ADVISOR TO CONSTANTINE I)

"Evil spirits being adjured by Christians, retire out of the bodies of men, confess themselves to be demons and tell their names: even the same which are adored in the temples [i.e. pagan idols]."

In later years, one of the reasons for the decline in activity of the Holy Spirit among the established Church, according to ST. JEROME, was that "The church lost as much of her virtue [power] as it gained in wealth and secular power."

An Introduction to Deliverance

REFERS TO

PIGS IN THE PARLOR CHAPTERS 1 – 4

PIGS IN THE PARLOR

STUDY GUIDE 1 · PIGS IN THE PARLOR 1

Resist the devil and he will flee from you – James 4:7b

The Christian should always consider indwelling demons as trespassers — one who unlawfully encroaches upon the territory of another. They are to be confronted on the basis of one's legal rights. We are the "temple of the Holy Spirit," purchased and redeemed by Jesus' work on the cross. Thus, the Christian should be assured that no demon has a legal right to indwell his body. A demon cannot remain when the Christian seriously desires him to go!

What would you do if a herd of filthy pigs came into your home? Would you pay no attention to them in the hope they would soon leave of their own accord? Would you try to clean up their mess as fast as they made it? You would do none of these things. You would drive them out as quickly and unceremoniously as possible! And this is to be our attitude toward demons. As soon as they are discovered they are to be driven out!

Questions for Review

1. What does the title of this book suggest to you?

2. What is the goal of demon spirits? Why?

3. What makes someone or something spiritually unclean?

4. Consider possession of land versus trespassing. What is the key difference?

Biblical Foundations

5. In Luke 4:33–34, a man with an unclean demon cries out before Jesus.

   a. What does he tell Jesus to do?

   b. Of what were the demons afraid in the above passage?

6. What do we learn about what happens to demons at Jesus' command? Why is this ironic?

   ➢ **Read Luke 8:30–31**

7. In Mark 9:17–18, what kind of demonic activity was occurring? Who was its victim?

8. Is there a relationship between deliverance from demon activity and the healing of physical bodies?

   ➢ **Read Luke 4:38–39**
   ➢ **Read Luke 13:11**

9. Read Matthew 12:43–44

    a. If demons are trespassers, how could they call your body their house?

    b. What character traits do these demons show by claiming your body as their house?

    c. In the above verses we are told that a demon finds no rest until he can reclaim a body to inhabit. What parallel to this exists in nature?

10. Read the account of the Gadarenes demoniac.

    ➢ **Read Luke 8:26–33**

    a. Could the man speak for himself?

    b. Who spoke?

    c. What did the man do to receive his deliverance?

    d. What does this say to you concerning the assumption that there are those who are unable to be helped?

11. Pigs and their herdsmen were Biblically unclean.

    a. What does the fact that the legion of demons was willing to enter the pigs tell us about demonic activity?

b. Given the demise of the pigs, what does this tell you about demons' spiritual knowledge?

12. In Mark 9:26, how did the demon leave the boy?

13. Given your answer to #12, why do you think Jesus agreed to allow the legion of demons to enter the pigs?

14. We have so far seen Jesus ministering deliverance in a number of instances. Was the casting out of demons a critical part of Jesus' earthly ministry?
   ➤ **Read Luke 11:20**

15. How central was the ministry of deliverance to God the Father?
   ➤ **Read the Lord's Prayer in Matt. 6:9–13**

16. It turns out that a measurable part of Jesus' earthly ministry involved delivering individuals from evil spirits. What does this say to the church and her pastors/shepherds?
   ➤ **Read: Luke 4:15–19**

17. Some groups decide not to address the need for deliverance within their congregations. Do you think that believers will be helped in their search for freedom if the pulpits ignore this topic?

18. How else can this information reach the people?

For Personal Reflection

19. What do you suppose has transpired in an individual's life by the time he or she seeks deliverance?

20. What does Hosea 4:6 tell you?

21. What does the following passage from the KING JAMES VERSION tell you about those who seek deliverance with honesty and sincerity?

> *And it shall come to pass, that whosoever shall call on the name of the LORD shall be delivered...*   –Joel 2:32 KJV

~~~~~ Key Revelations to Ponder ~~~~~

"Much misunderstanding has resulted from the use of the word 'possessed.' This word suggests total ownership. In this sense, a Christian could never be 'demon possessed.' He could not be owned by demons because he is owned by Christ."

— Frank Hammond

There is often an overlap between healing and deliverance. According to Frank Hammond...

"Healing and deliverance are companion ministries, for there are often overlapping needs. The epileptic may have a demon, but he may also need a healing of brain tissue. Whatever the need, we must learn to come to Jesus in faith, knowing that He is the Savior, Deliverer and Great Physician."

— Adapted from *Demons & Deliverance* by Frank Hammond

For many, knowledge concerning the topic of deliverance has been sorely lacking in Christian teaching. It is hoped that as you press forward into this material you will find the understanding you need on this vital topic.

Jesus said "These signs shall follow believers" and the first sign He mentioned was casting out demons. And yet Frank Hammond did not cast demons out of people for the first twenty years of his ministry. To learn why, watch a short video of Frank Hammond teaching at the following website:

www.impactchristianbooks.com/wiles

PIGS IN THE PARLOR
Answers to Chapter 1

1. Our bodies are temples of the Holy Spirit (*houses*). It is wrong that unclean pigs (*demons*) be allowed in.

2. Demon spirits aim to indwell human bodies; in doing so, they can more powerfully influence that person than when they work from the outside.

3. Exposure to, or participating in, sin or unhealthy conditions, whether physically and mentally. Also, sins within the bloodline.

4. *Possession* suggests total ownership, whereas *trespassing* denotes an unlawful occupant.

5. a. "Go away!" or "Let us alone!"
   b. Torment and destruction before the proper time.

6. They will be tormented in the abyss. This is ironic because the tormentors themselves will be tormented.

7. Muteness and epileptic convulsions or seizures. The victim was a young boy.

8. There is such a thing as sickness being caused by a demonic spirit.
   Luke 4:38–39 — Jesus rebuked a fever
   Luke 13:11 — A *spirit of infirmity* was the root cause.

9. Demons claim that your body is a "house"
   a. Demons make this claim through lies and deception. Satan is referred to as the "father of lies" in John 8:44.
   b. They show the desire to control and possess a living body, and to deceive the victim into believing that the demonic behaviors and thoughts are a part of the person.
   c. Parasites, such as ticks and leeches, must attach themselves to another living being in order to thrive.

PIGS IN THE PARLOR STUDY GUIDE

10.   a. No

b. The demon leader of the legion within the man which was comprised of 2,000 demons.

c. He fell at Jesus' feet in supplication

d. If Jesus delivered the most extreme case, then all things are possible!

11.   a. Demons can enter animals as well as humans.

b. Demons, as spirit beings, do not have all knowledge.

12.   The boy fell into "terrible convulsions" and appeared as dead. (NASB)

13.   He knew that loosing 2,000 demons at once could be extremely stressful for the man.

14.   If Jesus casts out demons by the finger of God, then the Kingdom of God has come upon us. Casting out demons is the basis for the establishment of the kingdom on earth. As light advances, darkness flees and individuals are then set free from demonic oppression and torment.

15.   "Deliver us from evil" is part of Jesus' model prayer to the Father.

16.   God's people, especially His leaders, should function in the same way that Jesus, our Great Shepherd, did.

17.   No.

18.   Deliverance teams meeting independently, and books and audio teachings on deliverance can help those who would not otherwise be aware of the topic.

19.   Often the individual is at the point of desperation because all else has failed.

20.   God's people perish for lack of knowledge.

21.   All who submit to Jesus (*call on the Lord*) can be delivered!

OUR SPIRITUAL ENEMIES

And these signs will accompany those who believe:
In my name they will drive out demons –Mark 16:17 NIV

All believers are, whether they acknowledge it or not, involved in a spiritual war. It is an age-old battle between light and darkness, good versus evil. The above scripture assures us that the believer in Jesus Christ has greater authority than the demons that oppose him. The power of the believer comes through the baptism of the Holy Spirit.

We today have the same authority and power for ministry that was given to the early Church. The *authority* comes through salvation; the *power* comes through the baptism of the Holy Spirit. The power given to the believer through this mighty Baptism is evidenced through the operation of the gifts of the Spirit, such as supernatural words of knowledge and the discerning of spirits. These gifts are indispensable in spiritual warfare.

Chapter 2 of *Pigs in the Parlor* describes the power of the believer that comes through the baptism of the Holy Spirit. In this Study Guide chapter, we will provide special emphasis on this baptism, because of the crucial role it played in Frank Hammond's ministry, and the ongoing role it plays in providing believers with the power for the deliverance ministry.

Questions for Review

1. Why is wrestling a good analogy for spiritual warfare?

2. What four things does Ephesians 6:12 tell us about our spiritual enemy?

3. Why has Satan made significant progress as he seeks to rule the world? And what can we do to stop his progress?

Biblical Foundations

4. At the cross, and following the crucifixion, what did Jesus accomplish? Why is this significant for spiritual warfare?
   - ➤ Read Col. 2:13–15

5. What does the following passage tell us?
   - ➤ Read Luke 11:21–22

6. Jesus reigns victoriously. Yet, what has to still occur?
   - ➤ Read 1 Corinthians 15:24–26

7. What happens to the enemy in the end? And who is involved in bringing about this outcome?
   - ➤ Read Romans 16:20

SPIRITUAL WARFARE

Although Satan has been disarmed and his armor taken, there is still a battle going on and we are participants in the fight!

8. Who helps us win spiritual battles?
   ➢   **Read Zechariah 4:6**

9. The following event occurred after Jesus' resurrection.
   What happened here?
   ➢   **Read John 20:22**

10. What did Jesus then instruct the disciples to do?
    ➢   **Read Luke 24:49**
    ➢   **Read Acts 1:4–8**

11. When was this fulfilled?
    ➢   **Read Acts 2:1–4**

12. To what did Jesus liken the Holy Spirit?
    ➢   **Read John 7:37–39**

THE HOLY SPIRIT COMPARED TO WATER

There has been much confusion in church doctrine concerning the baptism of the Holy Spirit. In John 20, the disciples received the Spirit. Nevertheless they were instructed to wait for the power of the Spirit to come upon them in Acts 2.

An excellent analogy of the two encounters with the Holy Spirit, in John 20:22 and Acts 2:1-4, is that of water and steam. Water and steam are the same element, however when water is heated it becomes a source of power (i.e. steam). The baptism of the Holy Spirit at Pentecost was the heating of the already present water of the Spirit within the apostles, thereby enabling them to manifest supernatural power for ministry.

13. What were the results of the Holy Spirit empowerment?
   ➢ Read Acts 2:4, Acts 3:1–10, Acts 16:16–18, & Acts 20:9–12

14. Paul was not one of the original apostles. Did Paul also experience Pentecost?
   ➢ Read Acts 9:10–17
   ➢ Read I Corinthians 14:18

15. Was the empowering of the Holy Spirit continued with other believers?
   ➢ Read Acts 8:14–17

16. List the signs that should follow all believers.
   ➢ Read Mark 16:17–18

For Personal Reflection

17.   Have you been baptized in the Holy Spirit?

Key Revelations to Ponder

The baptism of the Holy Spirit should not be a source of fear, but rather a source of exciting potential and power. Jesus makes a promise in the Book of Acts to His followers: power is coming to defeat the works of darkness. *"For John baptized with water, but in a few days you will be baptized with the Holy Spirit."* Acts 1:5

Note that in Acts Jesus doesn't "suggest" or "recommend" that His followers be baptized with the Holy Spirit. Rather, He "commands" that they should not depart Jerusalem, but wait for the promise of power from on high. It was, and continues to be, that important to Jesus.

—Adapted from "How to Receive the Baptism of the Holy Spirit"
in *Alive Again*, by Bill Banks

"It is not a time to pray that God will provide power and authority. He has *already provided* for our salvation, at the cross, and for our power for ministry, through the baptism of the Holy Spirit. He is therefore waiting for us to engage in spiritual warfare and become the militant church prophesied in Matthew 16:18 - to set the captives free!"

— Frank Hammond

Consider this verse:
The seventy returned with joy, saying, "Lord, even the demons are subject to us in Your name." And He said to them, "I was watching Satan fall from heaven like lightning. Behold, I have given you authority to tread on serpents and scorpions, and over all the power of the enemy, and nothing will injure you."   —Luke 10:17-19 NASB

OUR SPIRITUAL ENEMIES
Answers to Chapter 2

1.   It refers to close-quarter fighting, personally grappling with the powers of darkness.

2.   He is organized into Principalities, Powers, Rulers of the darkness of this world, and Spiritual wickedness in high places (KJV)

3.   He has not been adequately challenged by the Church, which has not fully risen up in the power and authority given it.

4.   At the cross, Jesus offered us eternal life, forgave all our transgressions, and cancelled decrees against us. He disarmed rulers and authorities. Our spiritual enemies have been defeated!

5.   Satan has lost his armor.

6.   Christ must reign until all His enemies are put under His feet. The last enemy is death. Then He will hand the kingdom back to the Father.

7.   Jesus will crush Satan under *our* feet. This means the Church will be actively involved in his destruction.

8.   The Holy Spirit helps us in battle.

9.   He breathed the Holy Spirit into the disciples.

10. Jesus instructed the disciples to remain in Jerusalem until the power (baptism) of the Holy Spirit would come upon them.

11. The disciples were filled with power on Pentecost (Acts 2:1–4).

12. Jesus likened the Spirit to water.

13. Tongues (Acts 2:4), Healing (Acts 3:1–10), Deliverance (Acts 16:16–18), and Resurrection (Acts 20: 9–12)

14. Yes

15. Yes

16. Casting out demons, speaking with new tongues, picking up serpents, not being poisoned, healing the sick

17. (Personal reflection)

FIGHT THE GOOD FIGHT

Put on the full armor of God, so that you will be able to stand firm against the schemes of the devil. –Eph. 6:11

The ministry of deliverance is first and foremost a battle for self. Does everyone need deliverance? Personally, we have not found any exceptions. While we have all walked in ignorance and darkness, the enemy has successfully made inroads into each of us. We must learn how to get him out and how to keep him out.

The second area of conflict in our lives is the battle for our families. In many homes today, even though husband, wife and children may profess Christ, there is strife, division, confusion, and chaos. It is time the devil took his share of the blame. And it is time families learn how to drive the devil out of their homes.

The third area of our lives in need of deliverance is our Church. Satan has a special interest in the Church. We can well believe that he will do everything in his power to sidetrack, hinder, weaken, and destroy the Church's ministry.

The final area of conflict is the battle for our communities. Hope for our communities and nation does not lie in social and governmental programs. Neither does it lie in education or science. Our problems are basically spiritual, and God has given us spiritual weapons and resources for victory!

Questions for Review

1. In the battle against Satan, "God has provided _____ for our protection and _____ for offensive warfare. Thus, we can withstand every assault against us AND launch an attack that will overthrow the enemy."

2. What is the first objective in spiritual warfare? What is an effective and necessary tactic for doing this?

3. A key point in this chapter is that warfare is not prayer, but we must be engaged in warfare, in addition to prayer. What is the difference, and why is the distinction important?

4. When we engage in spiritual warfare on behalf of another person, what will occur? What will not occur?

5. What are some examples of demonic forces that Satan utilizes to attempt to control local congregations?

Biblical Foundations

6. John describes the nature and activity of Satan. What does Satan come to do?
    ➢ Read John 8:44
    ➢ Read John 10:10

7. What are the pieces of our armor, and what does each piece represent?
    ➢ Read Ephesians 6:10–18

Now let us see how Satan attacks each of these areas of armor...

THE HELMET OF SALVATION

8. What lie does Satan tell to combat our salvation?
   ➢ **Read Ephesians 2:8–9**

9. With what does Satan assault our minds?
   ➢ **Read 2 Timothy 1:7**

THE BREASTPLATE OF RIGHTEOUSNESS

10. What tactic does Satan use to negate our righteousness?
    ➢ **Read Galatians 2:21 to 3:1–3.**

THE GIRDLE OF TRUTH

11. What do we need to guard ourselves against?
    ➢ **Read Colossians 2:18–23**

12. What does scripture say about membership in secret societies?
    ➢ **Read Matthew 5:14–16**

THE GOSPEL OF PEACE

PEACE

The Greek word for "peace" in Ephesians 6:15 is *elrene* which means "rest" — the absence or end of strife.

13. What is one way the enemy attempts to destroy our peace?

   ➤ **Read 1 Corinthians 1:10–13**

14. What would the enemy like for you to do in relationship disputes?

   ➤ **Read Ephesians 4:26–27**

"DO NOT LET THE SUN GO DOWN ON YOUR WRATH"

It is a fact that when you go to bed angry you wake up with resentment and resentment will become a root of bitterness if not cast out.

15. What does bitterness do to the body of Christ?

   ➤ **Read Hebrews 12:15**

THE SHIELD OF FAITH

16. What did Satan initially try to do in the Garden?

    ➤ **Read Genesis 3:1**

17. Would you say that this one verse from Genesis summarizes Satan's attack on our faith ever since?

THE SWORD OF THE SPIRIT

18. What is the Sword of the Spirit?

    ➤ **Read Ephesians 6:17**

A SPECIAL WORD FROM THE LORD

The Greek word "*Rhema*" is applied in Ephesians 6:17 and represents the Holy Spirit giving you a personal message to combat the "fiery darts" hurled at you. The picture of battle is clear. As Satan hurls doubts (fiery darts) you are to counter attack with the specific word or scripture the Spirit has spoken to you.

19. Can you think of an experience in the life of Jesus where He applied the weapon of the *Sword of the Spirit* against Satan?

For Personal Reflection

20. In Matthew 25:21, Jesus says that one must be faithful first in the small things before gaining charge over greater things. Can you relate this to the difference between personal deliverance and warfare for community and country?

21. In the following passage, what two words best describe Jesus' ability to cast out demons?

   ➢   Read Luke 4:31–36

ꙮ꙯ꙮ꙯ Key Revelations to Ponder ꙮ꙯ꙮ꙯

In Acts 1:8, the disciples were granted "miracle-working power." The Greek word in Acts is *dunamis* which means "miraculous power, might, strength." It is the Greek word from which we get the word *dynamite*! Does this help build your confidence to confront your own personal demons?

The Kingdom of God is defined as "*righteousness, peace and joy in the Holy Ghost*" (Rom. 14:17). Are you at peace? Do you have joy? Do you feel righteous? This is God's inheritance for you NOW! If you do not, there may be a demonic stronghold in your life.

Consider this verse:
"*our struggle is not against flesh and blood, but against the rulers, against the powers, against the world forces of this darkness, against the spiritual forces of wickedness in the heavenly places.*"   Eph. 6:12

Do you see the relationship between this verse, and Jesus' admonition to forgive our enemies?

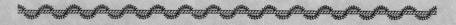

 # FIGHT THE GOOD FIGHT
Answers to Chapter 3

1. God has provided **armor** for our protection and **weapons** for offensive warfare.

2. The first objective in spiritual warfare is to free oneself. An effective and necessary tactic is to talk out loud to the demons (even though this may feel awkward at first).

3. In prayer we speak directly to God, offering thanksgiving and praise while seeking wisdom, revelation or solutions to challenges we are facing. In spiritual warfare, we speak directly to the enemy and command our freedom (or that of others), in Jesus' name.

    We do not pray to God for demonic freedom, because God has given us the power and authority to defeat the devil. In Frank's words, "We need to stop storming heaven for what has already been provided and start using what God has given us."

4. Spiritual warfare on behalf of another binds the power of demonic forces and releases the will so that the individual may make decisions apart from demonic interference. It does not, however, control the will of that person.

5. Spirits of strife; jealousy; obsession with doctrine, or human abilities; denominationalism; worldliness and materialism; formalism; ritualism; complacency; and discouragement are a few examples.

6. Murder, lie, steal and destroy

7. Helmet = Salvation
    Sword = Word of God
    Breastplate = Righteousness
    Girdle or Belt = Truth
    Shoes = Peace
    Shield = Faith

8. We are saved by our good works.

9. Fear, timidity

10. He tries to turn us away from Jesus and toward religious legalism as a source of our righteousness.

11. Individuals who would deceive and distract us from Christ through their false teachings and counterfeit supernatural experiences.

12. We are not to join. If these societies offer truth, then their teachings should be open to any person seeking truth, not just members.

13. By dividing the Body of Christ.

14. Let your anger settle into your heart, thus providing entry for the devil.

15. Bitterness causes trouble and defiles.

16. Satan caused doubt in the truth of God's Word, thus lowering our faith.

17. (Personal reflection)

18. The Word of God

19. The Wilderness Temptation

20. It is important to be set free from personal, demonic harassment before focusing your time on the larger issue of warfare in the heavenlies.

21. Authority and Power

THE VALUE OF DELIVERANCE

That he might present to himself a glorious church, not having spot, or wrinkle, or any such thing; but that it should be holy and without blemish. –Eph. 5:25–27

Deliverance is not a panacea or a cure-all. Yet it is to be greatly valued as an important part of what God is doing in relationship to the current revival in the Church. The Church is the Bride of Christ, and Christ is coming for His Bride. The scripture declares that His Bride must be cleansed. The Church for which Christ is coming is to be "holy and without blemish." Therefore, we must agree that unclean spirits must be purged from our lives.

Demons are enemies of the gifts and the fruit of the Spirit. They can keep these from coming forth in the Christian's life and thereby hinder the believer in his preparation for his Lord's coming. Freedom to live fully in Christ, then, is the great value of deliverance for the individual.

Questions for Review

1. According to the author, why do individuals come forward to ask for deliverance?

2. What means has the Lord provided by which believers can prepare themselves for the coming of the Lord?

3. How do demons hinder the process of preparation?

Biblical Foundations

4. Read Galatians 5:22–25 concerning the fruit of the Spirit. Fill in the chart with the provided space for the opposite of each fruit. The terminology in your translations may differ from the list, but use what your Bible lists as the fruit, and then write the opposite.

FRUIT OF THE SPIRIT	OPPOSITES
Love	
Joy	
Peace	
Patience	
Kindness	
Goodness	
Faithfulness	
Gentleness	
Self-Control	

5. In the case of the man in the synagogue tormented by a demon, what did the demon cry out?
   ➢ **Read Luke 4:33–37**

6. Can you think of a reason why the man was described as having a single "unclean demon" yet the demon said "we" in verse 34?

7. Why would a demon reveal Jesus' identity?

8. What happened to the man as he was delivered?

9. What was the value of this deliverance?

10. How was Peter's mother-in-law healed?
    ➤   **Read Luke 4:38–39**

11. What problems did the demon(s) cause the man in Matthew 12:22–28?

12. What word was used in Matthew 12:22 to describe what Jesus did?

13. Was the healing of the man in Matthew 12 also a *deliverance*?

14. Do these two scriptural examples reveal a close connection between healing and deliverance?

15. By what authority did Jesus cast out demons?

16. In this account, what source did the Pharisees attach to Jesus' deliverance ministry?

17. What was the judgment on those who called the work of the Holy Spirit satanic?

> ➢ Read Matthew 12:31–32

RESPECT FOR THE MINISTRY OF THE HOLY SPIRIT

There may be some who, because of never being exposed to an actual work of the Holy Spirit, are confused as to the source of spiritual power. This is different from those who actually see the Spirit at work and seek to hinder it by labeling it as demonic.

For Personal Reflection

The news about Jesus had spread beyond the borders of Israel, and to the Canaanites, who were known for their degenerate idolatries and enmities with Israel.

> ➢ Read Matthew 15:21–28

18.   Why did the woman approach Jesus in verse 22?

19.   How did Jesus refer to His deliverance ministry?

20.   What was it about the woman that inspired Jesus to attribute "great faith" to her?

Key Revelations to Ponder

Demonic bondages have been broken and lives liberated through the modern-day ministry of deliverance. And yet, as Frank Hammond states, "deliverance is not a cure-all." This is true in part because it is necessary to walk out freedom, to function in a new measure of discipline and self-control. Consider the words of Paul:

...but I discipline my body and make it my slave, so that, after I have preached to others, I myself will not be disqualified. 1 Cor. 9:27

The fruit of the Spirit is a special target for the enemy. The first and principal fruit is love. John says this about love...

The one who loves his brother abides in the Light and there is no cause for stumbling in him. 1 John 2:10

THE VALUE OF DELIVERANCE
Answers to Chapter 4

1. They come because they want to continue in spiritual growth and realize that every hindrance to spiritual development must be eliminated.

2. The Word of God, the anointing (gifts) of the Holy Spirit, and the fruit of the Spirit are all things believers can use to cleanse themselves in readiness for the coming of our Lord.

3. Demons can keep the gifts and fruits of the Spirit from coming forth in the Christian's life and thereby hinder the believer in his preparation for his Lord's coming.

4. The Fruit of the Spirit and their opposites

FRUIT OF THE SPIRIT	OPPOSITES
LOVE	HATE, RESENTMENT, BITTERNESS
JOY	DEPRESSION, MELANCHOLY, SADNESS
PEACE	NERVOUSNESS, ANXIETY, RESTLESSNESS, TORMENT, TRAUMA
PATIENCE	IMPATIENCE, FRUSTRATION
KINDNESS	SELFISHNESS, CRUELTY
GOODNESS	MORAL IMPURITIES OF ALL KINDS
FAITHFULNESS	ADULTERIES, SORCERIES, LYING
GENTLENESS	ANGER, TEMPER, STRIFE

SELF-CONTROL	SELFISHNESS, ADDICTIONS, COMPULSIONS

Note: your opposites may differ from the answer list; nevertheless can you see where the opposites of the fruit of the Spirit could become demonic in proportion?

5.   "Have you come to destroy us?" and "You are the Holy One of God."

6.   Others present in the synagogue also had demons and these demons knew of each others' existence.

7.   Perhaps out of pride; e.g. "I know who you are!"

8.   The man was thrown down and delivered, without harm to him.

9.   The man was healed, and testimony was given as to Jesus' authority. News about Jesus spread to the surrounding areas.

10.   Through deliverance: the fever was *rebuked*.

11.   He was blind and could not speak.

12.   Healed

13.   Matthew 12:24–26 suggest so: "...if it is by the Spirit of God that I drive out demons, then the kingdom of God has come upon you."

14.   Yes

15.   By the "finger of God" or the "Spirit of God."

16.   Beelzebub, the ruler of demons

17.   To never be forgiven

18. She cried out for mercy for her daughter, who was oppressed by a demon.

19. He compared deliverance to the "children's bread."

20. Persistence

HOW DEMONS MANIFEST IN OUR LIVES

REFERS TO CHAPTERS 5, 6, 20, AND 21 IN

PIGS IN THE PARLOR

DIAGNOSIS: *This section of the Study Guide will enable personal reflection and self-examination in order to begin a journey to freedom. Some of the answers will therefore be unique to your history and circumstances and are totally subjective. Some may be shared with a group, while others might be kept private.*

How DEMONS ENTER

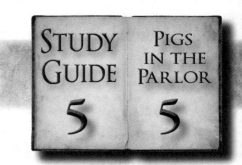

The thief cometh not, but for to steal, and to kill, and to destroy:
I am come that they might have life, and have it more abundantly. –John 10:10

Demons enter through "open doors." They have to be given an opportunity. In other words, one does not pick up a demon by walking down the street and accidentally bumping into one that is looking for a "home." However, Satan does devise a plan to ruin and destroy each one of us.

Doorways through which demons enter include sin, life circumstances, and inheritance. Some of these doorways are due to our actions and decisions of our will. Other doorways, like the circumstances that surround us and our genetics, are beyond our control. Jesus came that we all might have life, and have it more abundantly!

As we look at these three areas we need to remember that in addition to asking *how* demons enter we should also ask *when.* We will be looking at both childhood and adulthood for doors through which demonic bondage can begin.

Questions for Review

1. What is the relationship between the works of the flesh and the work of demons?

2. Willingness to forgive is given as an example. Explain.

3. When are doors are most commonly opened to demons in someone's life?

4. What did Frank Hammond's discover concerning his own "inherited" condition?

Biblical Foundations

5. According to Scripture, how long can a curse last if unbroken?
   ➢ **Read Exodus 20:4–6**

6. What kind of relief has Jesus secured for us against curses?
   ➢ **Read Galatians 3:13**

7. Can material possessions that we acquire, through inheritance for instance, carry with them a curse?
   ➢ **Read Deuteronomy 7:26**

For Personal Reflection

8. When do you think a person becomes responsible for their disobedience leading to sin (at what age)?

9. What are some examples of how demonic torment can happen in a child's life?

10. What demonic influences can enter into a teen's life specifically through exposure to violence, either through the media, peer pressure or gang influence?

11. Can you remember any exposure to the occult, to abuse or to violence in your own childhood? Do any doorways for demonic activity stand out in your childhood?

THE DOORWAY OF SIN

Children can be exposed either accidentally or forcibly to all forms of ungodliness such as pornography, sexual abuse, addictive substances, occult or cultic practices, or oppressive religious doctrine. Often parents are unaware that their child has been exposed to these things as this can happen through invitations from friends, at school, or when a child sees something in the media that he or she should not see. For a child, this would not be classified as "sin" but still leaves an open door for demonic attack.

Adults, on the other hand, may make conscious choices to rebel against godly instruction, to try various forms of addictive behavior (sexual or chemical), or yield to temptation in various areas such as hatred, wrath, envy, murder, etc.

12. What comfort does God offer concerning our sins?
    ➢ Read 1 John 1:5–10 to 2:1–2
    ➢ Read Isaiah 38:17 and Micah 7:19

13. Read 1 John 3:9 below. What is the key word that determines someone's willingness to sin?

    No one who is born of God practices sin, because His seed abides in him; and he cannot sin, because he is born of God. (NASB)

14. Can you see the difference between a sinner who consciously chooses to engage in sin and one who desperately wants to be free but feels controlled by compulsive addictions?

15. Which one will receive deliverance?

16. Looking back over your life can you name areas of demonic bondage to sin?

THE DOORWAY OF LIFE CIRCUMSTANCES

We have already seen some areas where life experiences in childhood and sinful choices in adulthood can lead to demonic entry. However, there are many other kinds of circumstances where children and adults can acquire demonic oppression.

TRAUMA

There are, for instance, certain traumatic life circumstances in adulthood which can result in demonic oppression. The enemy is an opportunist; often something such as an automobile accident can be extremely traumatic, leading to a *spirit of trauma*. There are, as well, individuals who have suffered the tragic loss of a loved one, suffered from physical abuse in marriage, or those who have undergone a divorce.

17. Children most often acquire demonic bondages through "traumatic events." Can you think of some examples?

18. Can you recall any of these types of traumatic life circumstances which have caused demonic torment in your present life?

19. What key does Romans 8:28 provide to deal with such experiences?

20. Can you think of a way that Romans 8:28 has been applied to your life? Are there areas in which you need to apply Romans 8:28?

INHERITANCE

21. Can you see the benefit of "Preventive Deliverance?" What do you think that means?

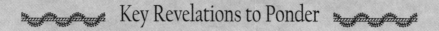 Key Revelations to Ponder

It is vital that we are *proactive* in our quest for freedom. There have been numerous cases where individuals were delivered of spirits of infirmities before they actually developed the symptoms! The person simply looked back over potential inherited conditions and sought deliverance from them in advance. Take time to reflect on any generational spirits, identify conditions that may be inheritable, and be proactive!

When praying against generational bondage, consider this verse:

"I know the plans I have for you," declares the LORD, "plans to prosper you and not to harm you, plans to give you hope and a future." Jer. 29:11

From the earliest days of casting out demons, Frank & Ida Mae Hammond learned to deal with demons of curses.

We have successfully delivered many Christians from curses. If it is possible for a Christian to have a demon, it is possible for a Christian to have a curse, for the power of a curse is demonic. When curses are canceled, blessings flow. Since you have God's favor, you are assured of His blessings.

Adapted from *The Breaking of Curses* by Frank Hammond

To see a short video of Frank Hammond teaching on the reality of curses, and how to break them, visit the following website:

www.impactchristianbooks.com/curses

HOW DEMONS ENTER
Answers to Chapter 5

1.   When a person yields to temptation he or she sins in the flesh. Through such sin doors can be opened for the invasion of the enemy.

2.   Unforgiveness can be an open door for demons to enter. For example, the unjust steward (Matt. 18) was turned over to the "tormentors" because he was unwilling to forgive his fellow servant.

3.   Doors are most commonly opened to demons during childhood. "The quickest way to understand what doors were opened for demons to enter is to hear an account of a person's childhood."

4.   He assumed he would have the same physical condition as his parents, only to discover that he could be delivered from these problems.

5.   To the third and fourth generation.

6.   Jesus took our curses upon Himself at the cross. Thus He has provided the power to break all curses on His people.

7.   Yes, some items we acquire carry with them curses. It is a good idea to prayerfully consider what we allow into our home.

8.   This is a difficult question: the transition from child to responsible adult may occur at different times for different people. In general, it happens in the early teen years.

9.   Often by accident, through seeing movies, TV programs, video games, Halloween haunted houses, or books which portray witchcraft or other occult practices. Also, through abuse and neglect from family members who have addictions or engage in sinful behaviors.

10.   Spirits of hate, murder, uncontrolled anger, or anti-social behavior

11. (Personal reflection)

12. Everyone sins, but Jesus Christ is our advocate with the Father when we confess our sins. God promises to cast our sins behind His back and into the depths of the sea.

13. Practice. Webster's defines "practice" as "to work repeatedly so as to become an expert."

14. One struggles to control his demons while the other ignores, or in extreme cases welcomes, their presence.

15. The one who desperately wants to change. The candidate for deliverance is obviously someone who does not want to continue to sin.

16. (Personal reflection)

17. Some examples include: being bullied or teased, feeling abandoned (such as in the loss of a parent or parents), accidents where the child is injured, or where he witnesses this happening to another, and parents or close relatives who manifest their own demons of addiction, lust or hate

18. (Personal reflection)

19. Romans 8:28 is the promise of a miracle. God promises to take the worst the enemy throws at us and turn it around for our good.

20. (Personal reflection)

21. Preventive deliverance involves casting out spirits of various infirmities common in your heritage before they take a strong hold on you. These could be both physical or mental.

SEVEN WAYS TO DETERMINE THE NEED FOR DELIVERANCE

Do not be deceived: "Bad company corrupts good morals." −1 Cor. 15:33 NASB

Demons are bad company. They corrupt good morals. How do we know if we are in need of deliverance? One way to know is when our morals (i.e., the fruit of the Spirit) are under assault. The symptoms of demonic oppression are usually on the surface, and are evidenced by a lack of self-control. The root of many demonic problems, however, lurk below the surface and usually wind up being a form of self-destruction.

Another way we can learn to detect evil spirits is by observing what they are doing to a person. For instance, a Syrophenician woman came to Jesus with an appeal that He cast an "unclean spirit" out of her daughter. The mother said to Jesus, "My daughter is grievously vexed with a devil (demon)." How did she know this? She knew it by the symptoms.

Questions for Review

1. What two principal methods enable us to detect the presence and nature of evil spirits?

2. Which of the two above methods represent the supernatural gifting of the Holy Spirit?

THE GIFT OF DISCERNMENT

The gift of discerning of spirits as described in 1 Corinthians 12 manifests itself as a supernatural "inner knowing." It can come by revelation to yourself, or through a deliverance minister. This gift is extremely powerful when looking for root causes of demonic problems.

3. What is the simple definition of "detection"? And how might a deliverance minister detect spirits?

4. What are the seven symptoms of demonic activity listed in this chapter?

5. What are some of the most common emotional problems?

6. What are some of the most common disturbances in the mind?

7. Describe some common speech problems that can arise from demonic influence.

8. List some of the manifestations of sexual problems.

9. What are the most common addictions?

10. What often needs to happen when spirits of infirmity are cast out?

11. What are the 4 areas of religious error?

12. What do "False Religions" include?

13. What do all "Christian" cults have in common?

14. How would you define Occultism or Spiritualism?

Biblical Foundations

15. The best counselor is the Holy Spirit. What role does He play in the diagnosis of spiritual issues?
    ➢ **Read Psalm 139: 23–24**

16. Willingness to _____ is essential to deliverance.
    ➢ **Read Matt. 6:14–15**

17. Is deliverance reserved only for a select few?

  ➢   Read Joel 2:32

For Personal Reflection

18. Can you think of an area in your life which falls into one of these seven categories?

19. Apart from deliverance, what steps can you take to fully renounce this unhealthy pattern of behavior?

Key Revelations to Ponder

"When we experience a pricking pain, we look for a splinter just under the surface of the skin. So too in deliverance, one looks for the source of discomfort, harassment, torment or fear just beneath the surface. The only real solution to a splinter is to undergo the momentary discomfort and perhaps even pain of facing it and digging it out. The same thing holds true in deliverance.

It is preferable to undergo the momentary discomfort, embarrassment or even pain to be able to be freed from the demonic source of a problem."

Adapted from *Power for Deliverance* **by Bill Banks**

Selfless, *agape* **love is the greatest antidote to Satan's hatred and pride. Consider this verse:**

Jesus replied: "'Love the Lord your God with all your heart and with all your soul and with all your mind.' This is the first and greatest commandment. And the second is like it: 'Love your neighbor as yourself.' All the Law and the Prophets hang on these two commandments."

Matt. 22:37-40

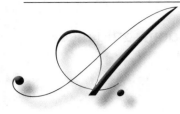

DETERMINING THE NEED
FOR DELIVERANCE
Answers to Chapter 6

1. Discernment and Detection

2. Discernment

3. Detection is observing what spirits are doing to and through a person. One might detect demonic spirits through a preliminary interview with the individual.

4. Emotional problems, mental problems, speech problems, sexual problems, addictions, physical infirmities, and religious error.

5. Resentment, hatred, fear, anger, refection, self-pity, jealousy, depression, worry, inferiority, and insecurity.

6. Mental torment, procrastination, indecision, compromise, confusion, doubt, rationalization, and memory loss.

7. Outbursts, lying, cursing, blasphemy, criticism, mockery, railing, stuttering, and gossip.

8. Fantasy sex, masturbation, lust, homosexuality, adultery, incest, provocativeness, and harlotry.

9. Nicotine, alcohol, drugs, medicines, caffeine, and food.

10. Prayers for physical healing need to be offered as well.

11. False religions, Christian cults, occult and spiritualism, and false doctrine

12. Eastern religions, pagan religions, philosophies, and mind sciences.

13. They deny or confuse the necessity of Christ's blood as the way of atonement for sin and salvation.

14. Any method of seeking supernatural knowledge, wisdom, guidance and power **apart from God** through Jesus Christ.

15. He can search the innermost part of our being.

16. forgive

17. All who call upon the Name of the Lord shall be delivered!

18. & 19. (Personal reflection)

DEMON GROUPINGS

*Or again, how can anyone enter a strong man's house and carry off
his possessions unless he first ties up the strong man?
Then he can plunder his house. – Matt. 12:29*

After your reflections from the previous chapters of this Study Guide, and before you move into the actual experience of deliverance, it would be helpful to read Chapter 20 of *Pigs in the Parlor*. This chapter identifies "strong man" spirits, and shows groupings of demons that can occur in a person's life.

It is important to note that as people read these lists of demons they may think that they have many of them. That is because our human nature is prone to these kinds of behaviors. However, what is necessary is to study these groupings and let the Lord, over a period of reflection and prayer, reveal which ones may have a demonic presence in your life.

One strong indication of demonic activity is when something is habitual or compulsive, and thus unresponsive to your own efforts to change. Quite often there is an undertone of addiction in connection to a demonic bondage, a stubborn bad habit that is not easily broken.

Questions for Review

1. What is a "strong man" in demonic oppression?

2. What two reasons can there be to identify such a ruling spirit?

3. What else does Frank Hammond say concerning ruling spirits?

4. Can similar demonic activity, such as extreme anger, be found in more than one grouping?

THE STRONG MAN

In Chapter 20, Frank Hammond offers more understanding on ruling demons, or "strong men" including Bitterness, Rebellion, Control, and more. Each is analyzed below:

BITTERNESS

5. How do "Bitterness" spirits operate in a person's life?

6. Is it possible to know if you have a spirit of bitterness?
   ➤ **Read Proverbs 14:10**

REBELLION

7. To what does the author compare a spirit of rebellion, and why does he state this?

CONTROL

8. In what cases does the author see unnatural "control" in operation?

9. Is it possible that a child could have an unnatural control over the parent(s)?

10. Define "witchcraft."

11. Does this tell you that a controlling person is assisted by a spirit of witchcraft even if that person is not aware such a spirit exists?

12. What kinds of spirits can enter a person who is being controlled?

WITCHCRAFT IN EVERYDAY LIFE

Often one of two methods is used in controlling another person. Either the controller uses anger and threats to get their way, causing obedience through fear, or he portends to be easily hurt if denied their wishes, causing guilt and fear of rejection.

RETALIATION

13. From what root do Retaliation spirits usually stem?

14. What phrase is a synonym for "retaliation"?

15. As opposed to a spirit of Retaliation, what does Jesus command us to be?
    ➢ **Read Matthew 5:38–42**

REJECTION

16. When does the spirit of rejection usually enter?

17. Can this enter even before birth?

18. What circumstances could lead to a prenatal spirit of rejection?

19. Why might adopted children have spirits of rejection?

20. What is the "three-headed" monster?

21. How do we know these are present?

22. Why is self-rejection a part of this group?

INDECISION

23. What behavior precedes indecision?

24. What other spirits are in the list accompanying indecision? (See grouping #24.)

25. What could cause a person to have the demonic problem of indecision?

26. How could a desire to control a situation be part of indecision?

SELF-DECEPTION

27. In what other ways does "self-deception" manifest itself?
    ➢ **Read Colossians 2:18–19**

A Self-Deceived Person

One of the greatest problems with this spirit is that the person having it rarely sees that it is there. It is, by its nature, deceiving. A person with this problem truly believes whatever he or she says, even if it contradicts something they had said earlier. Such people are often unteachable. One can never win an argument with them because they never see any wrong in themselves.

28. How could you tell if you had such a spirit?

PERFECTION

29. What spirit is usually behind a perfectionist?

30. Can a perfectionist be a controlling person?

31. What other emotions or qualities may accompany a perfectionist? (See Grouping #33.)

32. A perfectionist seems to be tireless in their attempt to perfect. Can you think of an opposite spirit that also can be there?

33. Who is the source of our perfection?
    ➢ **Read Philippians 1:6**

FALSE BURDEN

34. "Many believers need deliverance from false _____, _____, and _____ – those that are not from God."

35. In what kind of circumstances might we see this spirit in operation?

36. What is the purpose of this demon?

37. What does Jesus say to us regarding doing His work?
   ➢   **Read Matthew 11:28–30**

An Unnecessary Burden

Individuals who have this demon are usually overcome with the constant feelings of "should" and "ought," to the detriment of their own well-being.

RELIGIOUS ERROR

38. "Religious error is a broad designation embracing _____, _____, _____ and _____."

39. What does the Antichrist spirit deny?
   ➢   **Read 2 John 1:7**

40. What truth does Timothy tell us that serves as a foundation to avoid religious error?

    ➤ **Read 1 Timothy 2:5**

41. God warns us against participating in occult practices. What specifically are we warned against?

    ➤ **Read Deuteronomy 18:10–11**

42. a. Was the woman following Paul and Silas telling the truth?

    ➤ **Read Acts 16: 16–19**

    b. What did Paul discern as the source of her information?

    c. What did Paul do?

43. What do these demons of religious error cause?

Biblical Foundations

44. What caused Hannah's bitterness?

    ➤ **Read 1 Samuel 1:1-10**

45. a. What did the Lord call the Israelites to do to counter their rebellious nature?
   ➢   **Read Jeremiah 6:16**

   b. And what is the benefit to the soul that is stated in this passage?

46. When confronting a spirit of retaliation, what does the Bible tell us to do when we are wronged?
   ➢   **Read 1 Thessalonians 5:15**

47. Given your answer above, who can you turn to when you are wronged?
   ➢   **Read 2 Thessalonians 1:6**
   ➢   **Read Isaiah 54:17**

48. How are we to react when we suffer when doing right?
   ➢   **Read 1 Peter 2:20**

49. Numerous scriptures provide the antidote to rejection. Can you think of one? What comfort does this offer to us?
   ➢   **Read Isaiah 54:10, for instance**

50. What command did Jesus say to the judgmental perfectionist?
   ➢   **Read Matthew 7:1–2**

PIGS IN THE PARLOR STUDY GUIDE

For Personal Reflection

51. Is it possible to become bitter because of your own actions?
    ➤ **Read Matthew 26:69–75.** What happened here?

52. In cases such as this, whom do you need to forgive?

53. What pattern in your own life could possibly reflect a spirit of rebellion?

54. What overwhelming feelings would you have if you had been constantly victimized by a controlling person?

55. Have you experienced overwhelming feelings of the need to retaliate or seek revenge when wronged in various circumstances?

56. Are you carrying any false burdens?

Key Revelations to Ponder

Deliverance involves good detective work. While no two cases are the same, one learns to look for common threads of cause and effect. For instance, a woman who has had an abortion is susceptible to subsequent miscarriages and various reproductive infirmities. Seeing the effect, we can trace the thread back by asking if she, or someone in her recent generations, has had an abortion.

Witchcraft and control are often one and the same.

Witchcraft is defined as the manipulation, control, or domination of one person by another person. Unhealthy soul ties between individuals are often a form of witchcraft, to varying degrees. For example, if I were exercising witchcraft on you, I would be attempting to get you to do my will by a power that is not the Holy Spirit. This is the same as one person controlling another person.

     - **Adapted from** *Breaking Unhealthy Soul Ties* **by Bill and Sue Banks.**

Frank & Ida Mae Hammond encountered very few people who did not identify with the hurts of rejection.

When an inner wound is experienced, it must be immediately cleansed by applying forgiveness. Forgiveness is a spiritual antiseptic. When one is wounded by rejection, he must quickly forgive the offending party. Otherwise, an unclean spirit (a spiritual germ) can gain entrance to the wound and cause a spiritual infection called "demonization."

     - **Adapted from** *Overcoming Rejection* **by Frank Hammond**

DEMON GROUPINGS
Answers to Chapter 20

1. A "strong man" is a ruling spirit, or a group leader.

2. The Holy Spirit may be directing an order of procedure in the casting out of demons. Also, the knowledge of a ruling spirit can greatly benefit the person receiving deliverance as it will enable the individual to be alert for habit patterns that allow this kind of activity to reoccur.

3. They are often the first to invade an area.

4. Yes

5. Bitterness keeps hurtful incidents alive, poisoning not only one's own life but those around him or her.

6. Yes

7. A spirit of Antichrist, because rebellion refuses any authority, especially God's.

8. Parent over a child, one spouse over another, pastor over congregation, one church member over another or a group

9. Yes

10. Seeking to control another person by knowingly or unknowingly employing evil spirits.

11. Yes

12. Insecurity, inferiority, and fear

13. Bitterness

14. "evil for evil," or "an eye for an eye."

15. Forgiving, not revengeful

16. Childhood

17. Yes

18. An unwanted pregnancy, or failed abortion.

19. Because they were rejected by their natural mothers for whatever reason.

20. Rejection, fear-of rejection, and self-rejection.

21. The person has an inability to love or receive love.

22. A rejected person could decide that the problem lies with himself.

23. Procrastination

24. Compromise, Confusion, Forgetfulness, and Indifference

25. Fear of failure

26. To keep others waiting is a form of control.

27. Self-abasement (false humility) and false visions that do not originate from Christ.

28. One of the best ways to find out is to ask someone who knows you well, and can be trusted to speak the truth in love.

29. Rejection, or fear of rejection

30. Most definitely, and this is often the case.

31. Pride, vanity, ego, frustration, criticism, irritability, intolerance, anger

32. Fatigue

33. Jesus Christ

34. burdens, responsibilities, and compassions

35. Family, Church

36. To wear out the saints

37. His burden is light and His yoke is easy.

38. False religions, Christian cults, occult practices and false doctrines

39. That God has come down to us in the flesh

40. That there is only one mediator between God and Man: Jesus Christ

41. Human sacrifice, divination (fortune telling), witchcraft, and spiritualism of all kinds including associating with or acting as a medium.

42. a. Yes, b. A spirit of divination/fortune-telling, c. He cast it out.

43. Demons of religious error quite often cause:

    Mental confusion

    Dullness of comprehension

    Depression, fears

    Resistance to reading and understanding the Bible

    Spiritual hindrances to prayer, gifts of the Spirit, etc.

    Obstacles to the operation of the gifts of the Spirit

44. The constant taunting from Peninnah (Elkanah's other wife) relating to Hannah's barrenness.

45. a. Seek and ask for the ancient, Godly paths, where the *good* way is.

    b. "... you will find rest for your souls."

46. To not repay evil for evil but to seek that which is good.

47. Pray that God will vindicate you. You do not have to vindicate yourself.

48. Endure it with patience.

49. God's lovingkindness (mercy) will not be removed from us nor will His covenant of peace be shaken.

50. That he will be judged by his own standards.

51. Yes. Peter betrayed His Lord three times, and then realized his own personal failure and wept bitterly.

52. Yourself

53. (Personal reflection)

54. Guilt, Anger, and Hate are some examples.

55. (Personal reflection)

56. (Personal reflection)

SCHIZOPHRENIA

A double minded man is unstable in all his ways.
–James 1:8

The Greek phrase for double-minded literally means "double-souled." It is important to address this topic, not because you might have this disorder of schizophrenia, but because deliverance is quite often a battle of polar opposites, two minds at war. Experience has shown that if a person has one dominant form of bondage (the aggressive), he or she will also have the opposite kind of bondage (the passive).

As an example, a person with a spirit of *rejection,* which causes withdrawal from others, will often also have spirits of *rebellion* and *retaliation.* One side of the personality reflects severe internal wounding; the other side reflects outward anger and bitterness against others. Another example of this double-mindedness is the high-energy perfectionist or over-responsible person who also experiences oppressive periods of lethargy and fatigue.

Therefore, it can be said that most forms of demonization involve at least a small amount of double-mindedness in some form or fashion. As Frank & Ida Mae relate, "Almost every person who comes to us for deliverance is found to have varying degrees of the network of demon spirits which cause schizophrenia."

Questions for Review

1. As the Lord showed Ida Mae, the demonic spirits in schizophrenia must be _____, _____, and _____.

2. Why does the process of being set free from schizophrenia take time?

3. The constant conflict between the inward self and the outward self, each taking over in turn, causes what effect?

4. What characteristic is at the top of the list of the oppressed inward self, described at the bottom of the HANDS drawing?

5. What characteristic is at the top of the list of the oppressed outward self, described at the bottom of the HANDS drawing?

6. With what do the Hammonds say this conflict always begins?

7. What is the reactionary demon to rejection on the right hand?

8. Why are these two logically paired?

9. What evil spirits can cause a person to turn inward as a result of rejection?

10. Why do these come in?

11. Can you see why the spirits depicted on the left hand are reactionary to those depicted on the right hand?

12. What do the thumbs represent?

13. What is on the left thumb?

14. Why is this logical in a person oppressed by rejection?

15. What is on the right thumb?

16. Why is this person confrontational?

17. Does this individual have any regard for the hurt caused?

18. If you were ministering to this a person with this long list of opposing spirits, or if you had similar oppression, where would you begin?
    - ➢ **Read James 5:16**

19. What enables the real person (the one God created) to come forth?

Biblical Foundations

20. The controlling demon in the hands diagram is called Schizophrenia. How does the Bible refer to this condition?

  ➤   Read James 1:8

21. In Romans 7:25, Paul describes the conflict between flesh and spirit. Can you see how schizophrenia, to some degree, is symptomatic of being part of mankind?

For Personal Reflection

22. When we meet Jesus, we are recreated as glorious new creations. This our "Real Self." Can you describe some of the characteristics of your new, real self?

The Schizophrenia Revelation was at the center of the Hammonds' worldwide ministry of deliverance. Without this revelation, they said they might have given up in frustration. To learn more, listen to their commentary at the following website:

www.impactchristianbooks.com/deliverance

Key Revelations to Ponder

In our society today, "self" spirits are quite common, and strong. It seems one finds either unhealthy spirits of self-love and self-centeredness, or destructive spirits of self-hate. The Bible's answer for this is balance. A selfless love for Jesus, and a quickness to forgive, should bring us into a right mind to serve those around us. Ask yourself, "Are you a servant or a master?"

The schizophrenic-leaning person is always floundering ... "Who am I?" The identity of the true self is confused or lost.

The more serious schizophrenic deliverances require time — sometimes several months, or even a year or longer. The deliverance must work in balance with the development of the "Real Self." Identity with the "Real Self" requires time — as the schizophrenic nature is knocked out the true personality must come forth to replace it.

The most important thing in life is to know who you are in Christ. This means to know who your "Real Self" is, the one Jesus created you to be, when you became a new creation. Too few Christians know themselves in this light. This is the enemy's strategy to keep believers from becoming all that the Lord wants them to be.

SCHIZOPHRENIA
Answers to Chapter 21

1. Separated, cast out, given up

2. The process requires time due to the following reasons:

    It is a shock to the person to discover that so much of his personality is not the real self.

    He may be afraid to discover what his true personality is.

    He needs time to adjust and to fall out of agreement with the false demon personalities.

    He must come to loathe the schizophrenic personality, and fall out of agreement with it.

    As the person begins to experience deliverance, Jesus must start growing in the person, developing that personality, and making it what He wants it to be.

3. A hurricane in the soul

4. The inability to give and receive both God's and man's love

5. Inability to self-examine

6. Rejection

7. Rebellion

8. Spirits of rebellion compensate for those of Rejection. For example, a rejected individual can begin to lash out at those who reject him by refusing any authority, even Godly authority. He or she perceives that authority figures cause the pain of rejection.

9. Inferiority, insecurity, self-accusation, and compulsion to reveal weakness

10. Rejection causes a loss of self-worth.

11. Spirits of rebellion are compensating for spirits of rejection.

12. The Paranoid phase

13. Jealousy, envy

14. Rejected people envy those who have experienced satisfying love.

15. Distrust, suspicion, fears, persecution complex, confrontation

16. Internal pressure builds up as a result of the presence of envy and distrust causing the need for the person to lash out at another to relieve the pressure.

17. Usually there is no regard for hurt caused to others.

18. All help from Christ comes when we first confess our sins and seek forgiveness. This is a two-step process: confess the outward sinful behavior and deal with it, including confronting the areas where the person needs to forgive others. Then, pray for physical and spiritual healing.

19. When the individual learns to accept the new creation that Jesus brought forth, and begins to develop a solid trust in the love of God.

20. Double-minded and unstable

21. In our bodies there is a struggle between flesh (sin) and the Spirit (righteousness). Through the ministry of deliverance, and a life of active discipline, the outcome of this struggle should be heavily weighted to the side of the Spirit and righteousness. Are you being all you were created to be?

22. (Personal reflection)

THE PROCESS OF BECOMING & STAYING FREE

REFERS TO CHAPTERS 12, 15, 10, 7, 8, AND 9 IN

PIGS IN THE PARLOR

DELIVERANCE: *The goal of this portion of the Study Guide is to take the authority and power granted to you in the name of Jesus and break the demonic bondages in your life. Included are seven steps to enact your deliverance, then seven more steps to walk out your freedom, and steps to retain what you have received from the Lord.*

What is the goal each of us should have as believers in Jesus Christ? To reflect His nature more and more as time passes. We accomplish this by submitting to the ministry of the Holy Spirit and allowing God to transform us. One tool in this process is self-deliverance.

To watch a short video of Frank teaching on this, visit the following website:

www.impactchristianbooks.com/self

SELF-DELIVERANCE

*We ... are being transformed into his image with ever-increasing glory,
which comes from the Lord, who is the Spirit.* –2 Cor. 3:18

Self-deliverance is an important tool in the arsenal of an end-time Christian. It was Frank Hammond's conviction that a person cannot really keep himself free of demons until he is walking in this dimension of deliverance. The reason for this is that deliverance is a process. It would be nice if a person could get all indwelling demons out of himself and then forget about them for the rest of his life. But how many of us can keep ourselves completely free, especially in these lawless last days?

Naturally, there are challenges to delivering oneself. The biggest problem facing the individual is accurately *discerning* the spirits. Most persons are prone to confuse demon activities in their lives as merely expressions of human personality. It is not uncommon for a person to react to the discernment of a certain spirit with, "Oh, I thought that was just me!"

Then there are those who want to follow the do-it-yourself route so no one will know about hidden sins in their lives. This is not a good motive with which to begin self-deliverance.

As we mature in our walk with the Lord, we are also maturing in the art of warfare against the devil, as evidenced by our ability to conduct self-deliverance.

Questions for Review

1. Can deliverance be a "one-time thing?"

2. Who should we rely on to orchestrate which demons to address first?

3. In the Old Testament, were the enemy nations cleared away all at once?

➤   **Read Deuteronomy 7:22–23**

TAKING BACK THE LAND

Sometimes we need to hold our conquered ground for a season before moving into further deliverance. God not only wants you free, but to be able to hold your newly conquered ground.

4. What was God's desire for the next (and future) generations of Israelites?

➤   **Read Judges 3:1–2**

5. What incorrect diagnosis might you have when demonic spirits have inhabited your soul for a long period of time?

SELF-DELIVERANCE

There are some situations in which self-deliverance is workable and others where seeking help from others is recommended. This is a personal decision led by the Holy Spirit, but both options are valid. Unfortunately there are so few places where deliverance ministry is available that self-deliverance is often the only option. However, it is worth pointing out that deliverance ministries have seen effective results from praying over the phone with individuals who cannot be there in person.

6. What is the advantage of seeking a second party for help in your deliverance?

Biblical Foundations

7. Whenever possible, the Bible suggests seeking advice and counsel. Can you think of a Proverb that supports this?

8. However, a deliverance minister may not be accessible in your area. David was an excellent example of someone who sought the Lord directly for deliverance. What kind of encouragement does the following verse give to someone seeking self-deliverance?

> *Search me, O God, and know my heart: try me, and know my thoughts:*
> *see if there be any wicked way in me, and lead me in the way everlasting.*
> Psalm 139:23-24

For Personal Reflection

9. Have you ever practiced self-deliverance? What were the positives and what were the negatives of this experience?

~~~~~ Key Revelations to Ponder ~~~~~

Frank usually spoke to the demons in this manner:

"Demons, I know that you are there. I know of your presence and of your evil works. I tell you that you have no right to stay. I belong to Jesus Christ. Jesus purchased me with His own blood. This body is the temple of the Holy Spirit. Everything that defiles is cast out. You are a trespasser and you must go. I command you to go now in the name of Jesus."

A helpful hint: **when performing self-deliverance, stand before a mirror, look into it and address the demon in the authority Christ has given you. Command it to go!**

This would be a good time to begin to make a list of your deliverance needs, trusting the Holy Spirit to prioritize the list for you.

SELF-DELIVERANCE
Answers to Chapter 12

1. Not necessarily – it can be a process. It can be at times like peeling back the layers of an onion.

2. The Holy Spirit

3. No, they were cleared away little by little.

4. To also learn the art of war.

5. "Oh, I thought that was just me." or "That's just the way I am."

6. Confession to another keeps you from hiding or protecting that which is embarrassing to you, which may hinder your full deliverance. Also, a deliverance minister may discern something spiritual that would not be brought to light in self-deliverance.

7. Proverbs 15:22: "Without counsel, plans go awry, But in the multitude of counselors they are established," (NKJV) and Proverbs 19:20: "Listen to counsel and accept discipline, that you may be wise the rest of your days" (NASB) are two examples.

8. God is able and willing to discern our inner thoughts and to reveal our heart. He willingly serves as a discerner of spirits.

9. (Personal reflection)

BINDING & LOOSING

And I say also unto thee, That thou art Peter, and upon this rock I will build my church; and the gates of hell shall not prevail against it. And I will give unto thee the keys of the kingdom of heaven: and whatsoever thou shalt bind on earth shall be bound in heaven: and whatsoever thou shalt loose on earth shall be loosed in heaven. –Matt. 16:18–19

The Church, we are told in Matthew 16, is given complete authority over the "gates of hell." The Amplified Bible states it this way, "The gates of Hades shall not overpower it — or be strong to its detriment, or hold out against it." Thus, the Church is pictured as militant. Nothing can stop it — not even the forces of Satan!

It is no longer a matter of prayer by which we cry out, "Oh, God, please come and do something about this awful devil who is giving me such a hard time." But it is a matter of rising up in the *power* of the name of Jesus and telling the devil what he has to do!

The Greek word for "bind" in the passage before us is *deo*. It means to fasten or tie — as with chains, as an animal tied to keep it from straying. This is glorious! When Satan is bound he is made inoperable. He loses his ability to act against us. Jesus explains that He is able to control demon spirits and make them obey Him because he has already bound the strong man — Satan.

Questions for Review

1. Read the scripture quoted above. To whom was this discourse addressed initially? To whom is this discourse addressed today?

2. Does this scripture point to overwhelming defeat of the works of Satan?

3. Do we as individuals also have the authority from Christ to bind a spirit and loose ourselves from that spirit?

   ➤ **Read Mark 16:17**

4. Does the scripture in Matthew also point out that what we bind or loose here on earth has already been taken care of in heaven?

5. What does the Greek word for "bind" mean?

6. What does the Greek word for "loose" mean for us?

7. "The _____ refers to Satan and demons, and the _____ to the person who has been bound by the forces of darkness."

HEARING THE SPIRIT'S VOICE

Binding the evil spirits and loosing ourselves from them is an important start of our deliverance process. One of the blessings of this tool of binding the enemy is that it allows us to more effectively hear the Holy Spirit's voice and to better follow His guidance in the process of loosing ourselves from Satan's grip.

Biblical Foundations

8. When we bind the strong man, what can we then do to his house?
   ➤   Read Matthew 12:29

9. How did this concept of binding and loosing apply to the woman who was bent over and unable to stand erect?
   ➤   Read Luke 13:10–17

10.   From what was the woman in Luke 13 loosed?

For Personal Reflection

11. When she met Jesus, this woman was loosed from a debilitating spirit that had bound her for eighteen years. Does this give you hope?

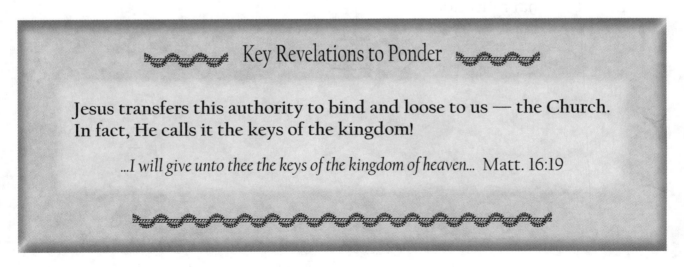

Key Revelations to Ponder

Jesus transfers this authority to bind and loose to us — the Church. In fact, He calls it the keys of the kingdom!

...I will give unto thee the keys of the kingdom of heaven... Matt. 16:19

BINDING & LOOSING
Answers to Chapter 15

1. First to Peter, but today to the Church!

2. Yes

3. Yes

4. Yes

5. *Deo* means to fasten or tie, as in a tied-up or caged animal.

6. *Luo* means to set free, to discharge from prison. Also, to free from bondage or disease by restoration to health.

7. Binding, loosing

8. Spoil or plunder it.

9. Jesus said she had been "bound" by Satan, and deserved to be "loosed" — even on the Sabbath.

10. A *spirit of infirmity* was apparently the cause of her condition.

11. (Personal reflection)

DEMON MANIFESTATIONS

When the crowds heard Philip and saw the signs he performed, they all paid close attention to what he said. For with shrieks, impure spirits came out of many...
–Acts 8:5–8

It is important to note in the above account that deliverance heightened the sense of attention among the crowd watching Philip. It says they "paid close attention to what he said." In other words, Philip was practicing a form of *deliverance evangelism*.

You will find that in situations where demons are being cast out of people in public that it can create an atmosphere of awe — as opposed to fear. There is an awe that descends on the unbeliever as they witness the power of God take control and dominate the power of demons. We have, for instance, witnessed salvations take place after a crowd saw a demon being cast out of a man with visible manifestations occurring.

However, on the other hand, some of the most powerful deliverances can have little or no manifestation. With regard to personal, one-on-one ministry, the magnitude of demonic manifestation can often be minimized by the candidate if they come prepared. In such cases, the demons may flee without a great deal of resistance and show. We recommend that a candidate prayerfully read a reputable book on deliverance, and make a list of the issues they want to deal with. Some people even chose to fast before coming for deliverance, although this is not required.

Questions for Review

1. Scripture indicates that in many of the cases when demons were cast out there were visible or audible manifestations.

   ➤ Read Acts 8:5–8. Who was performing the deliverances?

2. What was the manifestation that indicates that demons were being cast out?

3. Name a few of these manifestations mentioned in Chapter 10 of *Pigs in the Parlor* that stood out the most.

4. Demons usually exit through which parts of the body?

5. What was the demonic spirit Frank Hammond mentions that was responsible for the foul odor?

6. What demon was responsible for tearing the pages of Frank Hammond's Bible?

LOOK BEYOND THE MANIFESTATIONS

There are times in deliverance when there are virtually no manifestations. Much depends on the individual and the work of the Holy Spirit. We cannot predict what the reaction will be to a deliverance prayer. However, to receive deliverance, we have to be willing to go through temporary discomfort and unwanted display if it means being set free.

Biblical Foundations

7. What did Jesus do when a demon manifested in a man in the synagogue?

   ➤   **Read Luke 4:33–35**

8. In this example in Luke 4, what happened next?

For Personal Reflection

9. Most of the fear we encounter in people concerning deliverance comes from Hollywood. Many inaccurate and excessive displays of demonic power and disruption have tainted entire generations. Do you think these movies can themselves lead to spirits of fear?

10. As a deliverance candidate, are you prepared for the deliverance session?

11. As a deliverance minister, are you prepared to deal with the various manifestations?

~~~ Key Revelations to Ponder ~~~

Demons exist to torment and terrorize. Their most common defense tactic is to create fear in the hearts of deliverance candidates. It helps a great deal to remember that Jesus is perfect love, and perfect love casts out fear.

There is no fear in love; but perfect love casts out fear, because fear involves torment. – 1 John 4:18

It is clear that the Hammonds witnessed numerous demonic manifestations during their many years of deliverance ministry. For more examples of specific manifestations, and how the Hammonds dealt with them, read *A Tale of Two Franks* by Frank Hammond and Frank Marzullo.

When facing fear of Satan or demons, read Psalm 91 and Luke 10:19. Let these truths burn themselves into your heart:

I have given you authority to trample on snakes and scorpions and to overcome all the power of the enemy; nothing will harm you. – Luke 10:19

DEMON MANIFESTATIONS
Answers to Chapter 10

1. Philip the evangelist

2. Shouting with a loud voice

3. (Personal reflection)

4. The mouth or the nose or both

5. A spirit of cancer

6. A spirit of witchcraft

7. He rebuked the demon, saying "Be quiet and come out of him."

8. The man was thrown down, and then delivered without harm.

9. Spirits of fear are quite common in people who have watched terrifying movies, especially in situations where demonic manifestations are dramatized or exaggerated.

10. (Personal reflection)

11. (Personal reflection)

SEVEN STEPS TO DELIVERANCE

So if the Son sets you free, you will be free indeed. –John 8:36

One must practice honesty with himself and with God if he expects to receive God's blessing of deliverance. Lack of honesty keeps areas of one's life in darkness. Demon spirits thrive on such darkness. Honesty helps bring them into the light. Honesty requires a recognition that one is dependent upon God.

One must hate all evil in his life and fall out of agreement with it. This is repentance and renunciation. This means action — a clean break with Satan and all his works. Examples include destroying occult or pornographic material in the home, making the decision to stay away from friends who do drugs, avoiding or redirecting conversations in which friends talk poorly of their spouses, etc.

Willingness to forgive is absolutely essential to deliverance. God freely forgives all who confess their sins and ask forgiveness through His Son, and He expects us to forgive all others who have ever wronged us in any way.

These are the precursory steps to engaging in warfare against demonic powers.

Questions for Review

1. What is a good synonym for "light?"

HONESTY

2. What gives a demon the "legal right" to remain?

3. Demon spirits thrive on _____ .

EXPOSE THEM TO THE LIGHT

Demons can be likened to a fungus that grows in dark places. As long as we conceal their activity within us and make excuses for the behavior they cause, we cannot be set free.

HUMILITY

4. Humility requires a "complete _____ " with God's servants ministering deliverance.

OVERCOME EMBARRASSMENT

Take some prayerful time to reflect on any embarrassing problems in your life that may have opened doors to demonic entry. Also, recall embarrassing moments in your life, as these can often be traumatic and open doors to demons of fear and rejection. God can deliver you from the *spirit of embarrassment* and the painful memories of embarrassing moments in your past. What freedom we have in Him!

REPENTANCE

5. Can a person truly repent without a change in their lives?

6. "One must hate all evil and _____ with it."

7. What would hinder an individual's attempts to change, even though he or she has truly repented and striven earnestly to do so?

A SPIRIT OF SUBMISSION

Webster's defines "humility" as not proud, not haughty, not arrogant or self-assertive, possessing a spirit of submission.

MOVE FROM REPENTANCE TO DELIVERANCE

Many Christians repeatedly repent of the same sin. Because of the lack of knowledge concerning demonic compulsions or the lack of a deliverance ministry in their area, they never seem to get free. They are stuck in this step of the deliverance process. With knowledge of deliverance, they can press on and be set free!

RENUNCIATION

8. Renunciation requires action and a clean break. Give an example of renunciation for each of the following circumstances:

   A. Sexual addictions

B. Wrong sexual relationships

    ➤ **Read 2 Corinthians 6:14–18.** This should help reinforce the renunciation in the area of sexual sin.

C. Occult activity

D. Worry or anxiety, including fears

TURN FROM SIN

Repentance requires one to be genuinely sorry, while renunciation requires action — turning from sin and dedicating oneself to the amendment (change) of one's life. First repent, then renounce.

FORGIVENESS

9. Does forgiving a person mean that you must then lower your guard or trust them?

WISDOM IN FORGIVENESS

One can loan their new car to their son, but if the son carelessly damages that car, the parent most likely will not loan another one to him in the near future. To forgive the son is different from trusting him. The same is true for the business owner. If he finds an employee stealing, he can forgive him. But he would be wise not to offer him the keys to the safe.

10.   What do we learn about Jesus in the way He related to other men?
   ➤   **Read John 2:24–25**

Biblical Foundations

11.   What does Romans 13:12 tell you to do?

12.   Read 1 Peter 5:6–7.
   a. What two actions are required in this scripture?

   b. Why do you suppose these two actions fit together?

   c. What does Peter say will be the benefit of humility?

13.   Sometimes our human understanding of our circumstances can lead to worry and anxiety. Instead of leaning on our own understanding, what should we do?
   ➤   **Read Proverbs 3:5–8**

14.   Which should come first... deliverance or forgiveness?
   ➤   **Read Matthew 6:12–13**

103

THE LORD BLESS YOU...

You will find in Numbers 6:24–26 an excellent prayer to help you forgive someone. You can write this prayer, substituting a name to forgive into this blessing. Now would be a good time to list all those you need to forgive.

For Personal Reflection

15. Other than sin, what are other areas of enslavement that we might be embarrassed to face?

16. Can one be set free without complete honesty and humility in seeking help?

17. Can you think of any other form of renunciation you need to do in relation to your specific areas of bondage?

A Time to Pray...

If you have spent the necessary time in reflection allowing the Holy Spirit to reveal your problem areas and listing the order of attack, consider praying the self-deliverance prayer found in *Pigs in the Parlor*. It is presented on the following page:

Lord Jesus Christ, I believe you died on the cross for my sins and rose again from the dead. You redeemed me by your blood and I belong to you, and I want to live for you. I confess all my sins – known and unknown – I'm sorry for them all. I renounce them all. I forgive all others as I want you to forgive me. Forgive me now and cleanse me with your blood. I thank you for the blood of Jesus Christ which cleanses me now from all sin. And I come to you now as my deliverer. You know my special needs – the thing that binds, that torments, that defiles; that evil spirit, that unclean spirit – I claim the promise of your word, "Whosoever that calleth on the name of the Lord shall be delivered." I call upon you now. In the name of the Lord Jesus Christ, deliver me and set me free. Satan, I renounce you and all your works. I loose myself from you, in the name of Jesus, and I command you to leave me right now, in Jesus' name. Amen! [1]

---

[1] Used with permission of Dr. Derek Prince.

SEVEN STEPS TO DELIVERANCE
Answers to Chapter 7

1. Truth or Jesus

2. Any sin not confessed or repented of, including unforgiveness

3. darkness

4. openness

5. No

6. fall out of agreement

7. A demon – a "pig in the parlor!"

8. A. Sexual addictions

Destroying all pornography and abandoning sources of such

Refusing to listen to music or watch TV or movies with sexually explicit or implicit behavior — including unplugging from the Internet if necessary

Denying evil imaginations

B. Wrong sexual relationships

Ending all contact with these wrongful relationships

Ridding oneself of any objects connected with these relationships, including gifts and pictures

C. Occult activity

Destroying all literature and objects one has in this area

Refusing to read horoscopes, etc.

Refusing to watch movies or TV with occult themes

Refusing to listen to music that promotes occultism

D. Worry or anxiety, including fears

Cease studying or ruminating about possible medical, legal, environmental, financial, or political disasters, especially from media sources. It is next to impossible to believe God for something when the opposite is being fed into your mind on a daily basis. As much as possible, be selective about the company you keep and your media exposure.

9.   No. Pay special attention to the box labeled Wisdom in Forgiveness.

10.   He did not "entrust" Himself to any man. He exercised wisdom and constraint in his dealings with man. Proverbs 4:23 applies here: "Watch over your heart with all diligence, for from it flow the springs of life."

11.   To lay aside the deeds of darkness and put on the armor of light.

12.   a. Humility and casting your anxiety on God

b. To humble yourself by being honest about your bondages requires that you do not fear the response of God, nor fear His cleansing work.

c. God will exalt you at the proper time.

13.   Trust in the Lord with all our heart

14.   Forgiveness

15. – 17.   (Personal reflection)

SEVEN STEPS for RETAINING DELIVERANCE

So do not fear, for I am with you; do not be dismayed, for I am your God.
I will strengthen you and help you; I will uphold you with my righteous right hand.
–Isa. 41:10

Those who belong to Christ Jesus have crucified the flesh with its passions and desires.
–Gal. 5:24

Retaining deliverance requires a partnership between you and God. You are responsible for crucifying and disciplining the flesh. While you do this, God promises to uphold you in His righteousness. Deliverance does not mean perfection: you will still be required to live in *His* righteousness (not your own). But deliverance does mean freedom, the freedom to choose to walk daily in His will.

Often the battle for retaining one's deliverance is fought in the mind. Become watchful of any thoughts that could be considered negative; they are from the enemy. Separate those thoughts from your own. Refuse the thoughts the enemy gives you and replace them with positive spiritual thoughts. Confess what God's Word says, stay in the Word daily, and create an atmosphere of praise and thankfulness in your home, for praise silences the enemy.

Finally, stay in fellowship. It is the sheep that wanders from the flock that is most endangered.

Questions for Review

1. What are the seven steps for retaining deliverance listed in Chapter 8?

2. In Chapter 8 of *Pigs in the Parlor* Frank Hammond emphasizes the "helmet" (Eph. 6:17) as vitally important in retaining your deliverance. What part of the body does the helmet protect?

3. In light of this, what might Satan try to do to your mind following your deliverance?

Biblical Foundations

4. What does scripture advise regarding walking out your deliverance?
   ➤ **Read 1 Peter 5:8–10**

5. What does Jesus tell us to do in Matthew 16:24–26?

6. What does Philippians 3:13 tell us to do?

THERE IS POWER IN THE WORD!

It is important to read Scripture to receive strength against Satan's attacks. It would be helpful for you to journal those verses that seem to increase your faith. Also, acquiring a Bible promise book will help you find promise scriptures. What follows are a few scriptures to get you started.

MENTAL PROBLEMS

2 Timothy 1:7   1 Corinthians 2:16

ANXIETY

Matthew 6:25–34   Philippians 4:6–7

FEAR

Psalm 34:4   Psalm 56:11   Isaiah 26:3   John 14:27

ANGER/BITTERNESS

Ephesians 4:31–32   James 1:19

REJECTION

1 John 4:19   Luke 12:6–7

GUILT

Romans 8:1–2   Colossians 2:13–14   2 Corinthians 5:17

TEMPTATIONS

Hebrews 2:18

EVIL IMAGINATIONS

2 Corinthians 10:3–5

SEXUAL PROBLEMS

1 Peter 1:13–16

ADDICTIONS

Psalm 107:26–29

HEALING

Isaiah 57:18   Psalm 34:19   1 Peter 2:24   Psalm 103:1–5

For Personal Reflection

7. Read John 8:36. Does this build mental confidence?

8. Keeping this in mind, is it worth the effort to get free and stay free?

9. The seventh (and final) step in maintaining deliverance tells us to "commit yourself totally to Christ." Do you think that if you follow the previous six steps you will find yourself in total commitment to Him?

Key Revelations to Ponder

When faced with reclaiming areas of your mind following deliverance, consider the following verse:

We demolish arguments and every pretension that sets itself up against the knowledge of God, and we take captive every thought to make it obedient to Christ.
2 Cor. 10:5

Retaining one's deliverance from *mental illness* requires breaking the habit of negativity in one's mind. Following deliverance, this is accomplished mainly by replacing negative thought patterns with positive ones and promises from the Word of God. Hence we "take captive every thought" that stands in opposition to scripture. For more information on retaining one's deliverance, read *Tormented: 8 Years & Back* by Peggy Joyce Ruth.

 SEVEN STEPS FOR RETAINING DELIVERANCE
Answers to Chapter 8

1. The seven steps to maintaining deliverance are:
   1. Put on the whole armor of God.
   2. Confess positively.
   3. Stay in scripture.
   4. Crucify the flesh.
   5. Develop a life of continuous praise and prayer.
   6. Maintain a life of fellowship and spiritual ministry.
   7. Commit yourself totally to Christ.

2. The head and mind

3. Form doubts as to the validity of the deliverance

4. a. Be alert to the enemy's tactics.
   b. Resist the devil by remaining firm in your faith
   c. Remember, you are not alone; others have experienced the same troubles
   d. Be patient: you will experience the fruit of your deliverance because God Himself will...
      Restore you so that you are completely mended
      Strengthen and empower you
      Establish you (make you firm and steadfast)

5. To deny oneself and follow Jesus, in order to save one's life

6. Forget what lies behind and press on toward the future!

7.-9. (Personal reflection)

Filling the House

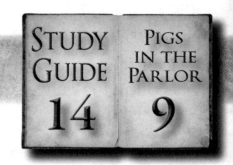

STUDY GUIDE 14 | PIGS IN THE PARLOR 9

Abide in Me, and I in you. As the branch cannot bear fruit of itself unless it abides in the vine, so neither can you unless you abide in Me. –John 15:4

We are told in plain language more than once that it is possible for a demon cast out to return, and even bring additional, more wicked spirits in with him. After the flesh is crucified and the demons are cast out, we must be filled with Jesus and let Him rule our lives. In fact, the reason for getting rid of demons is to be able to have more of Jesus! With what do we fill the house? JESUS!

How do we fill our lives with Jesus? By filling our lives with the fruit of the Spirit and with the gifts of the Spirit. For each demon that is cast out, the gifts and fruits of the Holy Spirit must replace it. This is the express responsibility of the delivered person. The deliverance minister should stress the fact that each person is responsible for filling his own house.

Questions for Review

1. What happens to demons that are cast out?
   ➤ **Read Matthew 12:43–45**

2. What do they desire to do?

3. What is the reason the above mentioned demons can re-enter the "house"(human body)?

4. In Chapter 2 of this Study Guide we examined the in-filling of the Holy Spirit as vital for our authority and power over the enemy of our souls. Following deliverance, we need to avail ourselves of what two aspects of the Holy Spirit?

5. Paul lists the nine supernatural gifts of the Spirit. What are they?
   ➤ **Read 1 Corinthians 12:7–11**

6. Why do demons despise these gifts of the Holy Spirit?

7. What are the nine Fruits of the Holy Spirit?
   ➤ **Read Galatians 5:22–23**

8. This fruit comes by abiding in the Vine (Jesus). What does this mean?

9. What was the key to Mr. A's remarkable deliverance?

10. What was the activity of the "torment" spirit in Mrs. B's mind?

11. How did she finally close the door to the demonic fear and anxiety?

Biblical Foundations

12. What is the work of the Spirit which can bring the joy back into our lives?
     ➢ **Read Isaiah 61:1–3**

13. Frank Hammond tells us to stay in praise and prayer to find our peace. What precedes the Godly gift of peace?
     ➢ **Read Philippians 4:6–7**

For Personal Reflection

14. What happens when we fellowship with like-minded believers?
     ➢ **Read 1 John 1:7**

FELLOWSHIP WITH LIKE-MINDED BELIEVERS

It is important to note that there are various avenues of fellowship; ranging from a small prayer/Bible study group (of 2 or more) to conferences and meetings, as well as regular church services. Ask the Holy Spirit to assist you in finding a place where you can fellowship with true Christian friends. This usually happens in small group settings, whereas church services assist us in worship and instruction. Both are beneficial.

 Key Revelations to Ponder

Demons despise the gifts of the Holy Spirit and cause men to despise them. Why? Because the operation of these supernatural gifts of power *counters* the work of demons. For instance, the presence of demons and their specific wiles are exposed by the *discerning* of spirits and the word of *knowledge*.

The fruit of the Spirit is not produced by independent action or by personal effort: it only comes by abiding in the Vine! What we are after through deliverance is to cast out the demons and their influence in order to replace them with Jesus and the fruit of the Spirit. Unless one understands this and makes it a definite goal, whatever benefits one gains through deliverance will eventually be lost.

FILLING THE HOUSE
Answers to Chapter 9

1. They enter into dry, waterless places seeking rest, and cannot find it.

2. Find a place to rest and occupy

3. It is empty, swept clean and *unoccupied.*

4. Gifts (power) and Fruit (purity)

5. The nine gifts of the Spirit, with explanation, include:

    1. WORD OF WISDOM - Divine wisdom tells you what would God say about a situation, what would He do, and how would He do it.

    2. WORD OF KNOWLEDGE - God reveals something to you to help or enlighten a situation through Knowledge. A word of Knowledge is a fact that God gives you regarding a situation, a word of Wisdom is how to apply this fact from the word of Knowledge!

    3. FAITH - This is faith beyond what we usually have in our walk with Christ, a faith to perform great acts.

    4. GIFTS OF HEALING - This is a supernatural empowerment to pray for the sick.

    5. WORKING OF MIRACLES - These are other miraculous works, for instance when Jesus changed water into wine.

    6. PROPHECY - This is God speaking through an individual to edify or warn the Church.

    7. DISCERNING OF SPIRITS - This gift is meant to discern what are evil spirits, human spirits, and the Holy Spirit.

    8. KINDS OF TONGUES - Each person can have his unique, private prayer language in order to let the Holy Spirit assist in prayer beyond one's own understanding; to edify himself or the church. Then there is the public gift of tongues for the whole Body.

    9. INTERPRETATION OF TONGUES - To allow knowledge of what the Spirit said in the utterance of the tongue.

6.   The operation of these gifts counter the work of demons.

7.   The nine Fruits of the Spirit are:
    1. Love (1 Corinthians 13 is a good reference for this.)
    2. Joy
    3. Peace
    4. Longsuffering/Patience
    5. Kindness
    6. Goodness/Moral Purity
    7. Faithfulness, Loyalty
    8. Meekness/Gentleness
    9. Temperance/Self-Control

(Different translations may use different words, but the meaning is the same.)

8.   Stay connected with Jesus so that the life of Christ will flow into the branches (us) and produce fruit.

9.   Forgiveness

10.   It was creating a crisis in her mind that did not exist in reality.

11.   Through faith and trust in God's love and protection

12.   Isaiah 61:1–3 lists the following ministries of the Holy Spirit:

    1. Bind up the brokenhearted.
    2. Comfort those who mourn.
    3. Grant beauty for ashes.
    4. Give the oil of gladness for the spirit of mourning.
    5. Grant the garment of praise in place of the spirit of heaviness.

13.   Prayer, petition, and thanksgiving

14.   There are many benefits, including support and encouragement as we "fill our house." 1 John 1:7 says that as we walk in the light, and fellowship with one another, the "blood of Jesus purifies us from all sin."

Section IV

Setting Others Free:

The Deliverance Ministry

Refers to

Chapters 18, 22, 11, 17, 19, 16, 14, 13, and 23 in

Pigs in the Parlor

ENGAGING IN THE MINISTRY: *All of us can pray for one another for healing. Similarly, we can pray for one another for deliverance! This is part of the walk of an effective Christian. Yet, the question as to whether you should become a full-time deliverance minister requires some investigation. This section will take you through the requirements, as well as answer some of the more pressing questions about the deliverance ministry.*

SHOULD I BE A DELIVERANCE MINISTER?

"Heal the sick, raise the dead, cleanse the lepers, cast out demons. Freely you received, freely give."
–Matt. 10:8

We should all be in a position, spiritually, to minister to others. This is an essential part of keeping the Body of Christ healthy and protected. However, the specific question as to whether you should become a deliverance minister requires some investigation. As Frank Hammond often relates, "If you look outside on the ground you will find furrows made by my toes when I was being dragged into this business." This is a common testimony of many deliverance ministers.

Being an effective deliverance minister requires heart. You need to be able to sympathize with the tragedies, and take joy in the triumphs, all while guarding your heart. You have to have the time and energy to treat each candidate as unique. It is a great help to have life experiences to bring to the ministry; you have to be able to relate to the candidate and their problems. Someone in their forties, for instance, should have lived through more rejection, rebellion, lust, or fear than someone in their twenties. Wisdom often comes with age. All that being said, it is ultimately the power and might of the Holy Spirit that brings freedom from bondage (Zech. 4:6).

Do not let fear guide you in this decision. Fear prevents many from becoming deliverance ministers, both the fear of demons and the fear of men. Instead, let the Holy Spirit lead.

Questions for Review

1. Frank Hammond describes his first encounter with the ministry of deliverance. How did he come to the realization that his friend's problem was a demon?

2. Did it surprise you that an incident in the natural (a head injury) could cause demonic activity within his body?

3. What adverse thought entered Frank Hammond's mind when he considered praying deliverance for his friend?

4. Even though Fred experienced deliverance when he and his wife first prayed with the Hammonds, why was he not fully set free?

5. What is the main hindrance to people wanting to enter the deliverance ministry?

6. Frank Hammond lists four qualities of a deliverance minister. What are they?

Biblical Foundations

7. Read Luke 10:17–20 and Revelation 12:7–11. What does this tell you?

8. What three things led to Satan's defeat?
   ➤ **Read Revelation 12:11**

9. The third point in Revelation 12:11 requires sacrifice on our part. What are the three personal demands made upon the deliverance minister?

10. Obviously Paul struggled with his own past sins and imperfections. Did Paul reach perfection before casting out demons?
    ➤ Read 1 Corinthians 15:9 and Romans 7:18–19

11. When will we finally be perfect?
    ➤ Read Hebrews 12:22–23

For Personal Reflection

12. What are some of the blessings and benefits (joys) of this ministry, as Frank Hammond describes them?

Key Revelations to Ponder

The freer we become individually, the more able we are to help others. However, if ministry required us to be completely perfect, we could never minister to anyone! Our perfection is an ongoing process. Take encouragement from Philippians 1:6:

"He who began a good work in you will perfect it until the day of Christ Jesus." (NASB)

Frank notes: "I have often commented that one of the greatest blessings that has come to me through this ministry is the insight I have gained into the spiritual realm. Spiritual awareness is quickened. Satan's wiles are much more readily discerned. The path of righteousness before God is plainer than it ever was."

SHOULD I BE A DELIVERANCE MINISTER?
Answers to Chapter 18

1. Revelation from the Holy Spirit

2. (Personal reflection)

3. He might become a target for demons himself.

4. There was another spirit present — pain.

5. Fear of Satan and demons, and the fear of man's opinion.

6. The four characteristics necessary in a deliverance minister are:
   1. Loving & wise, having genuine compassion for others
   2. Free from blame — personally free of demonic influence
   3. Willing to bear another's burdens
   4. Willing to spend time in prayer and fasting (especially prior to a deliverance session)

7. That Satan has already been overcome.

8. The blood of the Lamb, the word of our testimony, the willingness to sacrifice our lives if necessary.

9. Time, Energy, Patience

10. No

11. In heaven

12. The joy of seeing the Holy Spirit at work through us
    The joy of seeing captives set free
    The joy of receiving revelation of the spiritual realm
    (Personal reflection)

FACING AND ISSUES QUESTIONS

If any of you lacks wisdom, let him ask of God, who gives to all liberally and without reproach, and it will be given to him.
–James 1:5

When a decision is made to become involved in the deliverance ministry one is confronted with questions and issues. There are some things about demons and deliverance that one would be unwise to be dogmatic about. And then there are some questions for which no complete answers can be found. Such is the nature of warfare.

However, there are some common questions which arise in the ministry of deliverance that deserve solid answers. As you have progressed through this Study Guide you have already found answers to many of these questions and issues. Now would be an appropriate time to review some of the more important ones listed in Chapter 22 of *Pigs in the Parlor*.

For instance, "How can a demon spirit indwell the same body at the same time as the Holy Spirit?" "Can a non-Christian be delivered?" "Is this a wise thing to do?" and "Can we forbid demons to re-enter a person?" And so forth. Here we find answers to some of the most frequently asked questions regarding deliverance.

Questions for Review

AREN'T WE LESS EFFECTIVE THAN JESUS?

1. What affected Frank Hammond's ability to move against Satan with increasing authority?

2. How does one gain experience in this kind of ministry?

How Can a Christian Have Demons?

3. What parts of the human being does the demon inhabit?

4. What three elements comprise the soul?

Can a Non-Christian be Delivered?

5. What was Frank Hammond's answer to this question?

6. Why, then, does he doubt the wisdom of delivering a non-believer?

Salvation & Deliverance

A tormented person coming for help needs to first be confronted with the knowledge of salvation through Jesus Christ. These individuals usually understand salvation and are willing to accept Jesus as their savior prior to the deliverance session. There are extreme cases where the individual cannot comprehend salvation teaching because of the level of demonic torment (as in the case of the Gadarene demoniac). Nevertheless he or she can know they need help as we saw when the Gadarene demoniac fell at the feet of Jesus. In cases such as these, some deliverance may be needed prior to praying for salvation; but where the candidate stands with Christ has to be addressed at some point in the deliverance session! Following the session it is advisable to offer the baptism of the Holy Spirit to enable the person to "fill his house" and remain free.

What Happens to Demons that are Cast Out?

7. Can demons find rest apart from inhabiting an earthly body?
    ➢   **Read Matthew 12:43–45**

8. Where do they "walk" as they try to find rest?

Can We Tell Demons Where to Go?

9. Does scripture authorize us to impose premature torment upon demons?
    ➢   **Read Matthew 8:29**

10. Why were the demons sent into swine?
    ➢   **Read Mark 5:10**

Can We Forbid Demons to Re-Enter a Person?

11. What was exceptional about the deliverance of the boy in Mark 9:25?

12. What does Frank Hammond say concerning the forbidding of demons to return?

13. Is it ever possible to forbid the re-entry?

SHOULD HOUSES BE CLEANSED OF EVIL SPIRITS?

14. Can demons be attached to objects? What are some examples?
    ➤ **Read 1 Corinthians 10:19–21**

IDOLS IN THE HOME

One of the best definitions of "idol" is in Webster's Dictionary: "an object of passionate devotion." One can have idols as mere artifacts or "souvenirs" but devotion to them represents an unhealthy soul-tie. Other items carry with them a history of being worshipped, even if they are merely for decoration. Hence they may have demonic power.

15. Wouldn't it make perfect sense to remove or destroy objects representing Satanic worship, doctrine, or immorality from a home?
    ➤ **Read Acts 19:19**

IS IT NECESSARY TO CALL DEMONS OUT BY SPECIFIC NAMES?

16. If a demon's name is not discerned, what will usually cause a demon to respond and leave?

17. What is the main value in knowing either the names or specific defining activity of the demons you are confronting?

Biblical Foundations

18. What are we promised in John 14:12?

ABUNDANT, MIGHTY POWER

The Greek word *megas* in John 14:12 is translated as "greater" and can mean both "all the more abundant" or "mightier." Either way, we are promised both the anointing and authority to proceed in our ministry as Jesus did.

19. In 3 John 1:2, is John's prayer directed at believers or unbelievers?

20. Is the real question, *can* a non-Christian be delivered, or *should* a non-Christian be delivered?
> **Read Matthew 12:43-45**

For Personal Reflection

21. Can you define the difference between a Christian soul with natural imperfections and one with problems of a demonic nature?

~~~~~~ Key Revelations to Ponder ~~~~~~

Our hearts are grieved by those who contend that Christians cannot have demons, thus robbing believers of a valid ministry purchased for us by the blood of Jesus. This misplaced theology is one of the greatest obstacles to the Church being washed and cleansed, and individuals experiencing the peace, joy and righteousness of the Kingdom of God.

The answer is made clear by remembering that "your body is a temple of the Holy Spirit" (1 Cor. 6:19). The Temple in Jerusalem had three parts: the Outer Court, the Holy Place and the Holy of Holies. The presence of God dwelt solely in the Holy of Holies.

Jesus, however, found defilement in the Jerusalem temple. The money changers and the merchants with doves and cattle were not in the Holy of Holies, but in the outer courts of the temple. Jesus proceeded to "cast out" all who defiled the temple.

This is a perfect analogy to deliverance. Defilement is not in the spirit of a Christian but in the "outer courts" of his mind, emotions and body. There can be defilement in the Outer Court while the presence of the Lord remains in the Holy of Holies. Jesus is highly displeased with such a condition. He wants His temple cleansed and every defiling demon cast out.

Compiled from *A Manual for Children's Deliverance*, by Frank Hammond

FACING ISSUES & QUESTIONS
Answers to Chapter 22

1. Increasing experience in this ministry

2. By simply stepping out and beginning. The Holy Spirit will enable you to learn as you go.

3. The soul and body

4. Mind, will, and emotions

5. Yes

6. There are three reasons Frank Hammond cites:

    1. There is no hope of keeping the demons out, because the person is not submitted to Jesus and the Holy Spirit.

    2. You could do the person more harm than good because the unclean spirit can return and bring additional, more wicked spirits.

    3. The person's motive would be only selfish, and not for the glory of, and dedication to, God.

7. No. Demons are parasites; they can only draw their life from indwelling a host.

8. They walk through dry places in search of rest.

9. No — that time is fixed by the counsel of God.

10. For two reasons. First, they requested the pigs as hosts. Second, because of the large number of demons (legion) inhabiting the man, Jesus protected him from the violent force of the deliverance on his body.

11. Jesus forbade the demon to return because the candidate was a child who was not fully covered by the faith of the parent.

12. This would eliminate the need for the believer to stay free, which is necessary by the strengthening of his or her will (not the will of the deliverance minister).

13. Yes — by revelation of the Holy Spirit.

14. Demons can be attached to idols, certain books, charms, and visual media.

15. Yes

16. Demons will usually respond to a description of what they are causing.

17. Demons hate being drawn into the light, and being exposed in name or description causes them to leave sooner in some cases. Knowing their name also provides the person being delivered with the knowledge of what he or she needs to continue to resist, and provides clues as to the attitudes and practices that need to change.

18. That we would do greater works because Jesus was going back to the Father.

19. Believers

20. The question is *should* a non-Christian be delivered? Why subject a repentant unsaved person to more torment?

21. An elevated level of torment combined with a frustrated inability to become free, even after constant prayer, are sure indications that deliverance is needed!

DELIVERANCE
INDIVIDUAL & GROUP
PRIVATE & PUBLIC

...on the sabbath day he entered into the synagogue, and taught...
And there was in their synagogue a man with an unclean spirit, and he cried out...
And Jesus rebuked him saying, Hold thy peace, and come out of him.
–Mark 1:21,23,25

Deliverance CAN take place as part of a regular church service or other group ministry settings. Jesus did not shrink back from casting out demons publicly and in the place of worship and teaching. The very presence of those who are moving in the power of God can often cause demonic spirits to react and cry out or speak out.

When schedules allow, however, it is usually preferable to arrange for a private deliverance session, one-on-one with the individual or candidate. This allows private sins to be aired in a confidential environment. Nonetheless, Frank Hammond points out that there are many ways in which the ministry of deliverance can be conducted, based on scriptural examples.

It is inconceivable that Jesus ministered to each person individually. He was swarmed by multitudes of persons wanting healing and deliverance everywhere He went, yet the record makes it clear that he ministered to "all" who came. So clearly there is both need and example given in Scripture for individual and group ministry.

Questions for Review

1. Chapter 11 of *Pigs in the Parlor* describes three kinds of settings in which deliverance can happen. What are they?

HEALING & DELIVERANCE

One kind of church service can merge into the other; just as healing and deliverance are closely connected. Be prepared to address the deliverance issues that arise!

2. "Deliverance belongs to the Church. It should go right along with _____ , _____, and _____ ."

3. Why must the Church be active in the ministry of deliverance?

4. Sometimes demons interrupt Church services and cry out. Why does this happen?

5. The one-on-one conference-type of ministry has the disadvantage of being _____ , but the advantage of being _____.

Biblical Foundations

6. Did Jesus cast out demons in private or pubic?
   ➢ Read Matthew 4:23–24 and 8:16

For Personal Reflection

7.   What method — individual or group — is likely to be the most beneficial for the tormented individual?

 Key Revelations to Ponder

The ministry of deliverance belongs to the church. It should go right along with preaching, teaching, and healing. It is important that the deliverance minister be prepared to respond in any setting if the need arises. Jesus, our model, did not shy away from casting out demons publicly and in the place of worship and teaching (the synagogues).

The heart of Jesus cries out for more workers. In the context of Matthew 10, Jesus is engaged in His ministry of teaching, preaching, healing and *CASTING OUT DEMONS*. In this context He says...

The harvest truly is plenteous, but the labourers are few; pray ye therefore the lord of the harvest, that he will send forth labourers into his harvest. Matt. 9:36-38

 # DELIVERANCE: INDIVIDUAL & GROUP, PUBLIC & PRIVATE
Answers to Chapter 11

1. Deliverance can take place in the following three settings:

   a. Demons can manifest their interruptive presence in a regular church service and need to be dealt with at that time, or shortly thereafter.

   b. During private sessions with the deliverance candidate

   c. During public services dedicated strictly to a deliverance session, just as there can be services devoted to physical healing

2. Preaching, teaching and healing

3. To be prepared for the coming of Lord Jesus

4. The very presence of the power of God among the believers cause the spirits to react or cry out.

5. time-consuming; more thorough.

6. It is possible that both happened.

7. (Personal reflection)

THE DELIVERANCE TEAM

*Again I say to you, that if two of you agree on earth about anything that they may ask,
it shall be done for them by My Father who is in heaven.*
−Matt. 18:19

Jesus established the pattern of teamwork for His disciples. When He sent the twelve out in ministry He sent them two by two. When He commissioned the seventy He also sent them out two by two. In general, we always suggest that a second person from the ministry team be on hand during deliverance, whether they are active in the session or not.

How many should ideally compose a deliverance team? This cannot be answered arbitrarily. The situations for deliverance vary. What is certain is that there must be unity in the team, and a degree of flexibility to allow for the Holy Spirit to work.

Questions for Review

1. What is an appropriate range of size for a deliverance team?

2. What is absolutely essential for a deliverance team?

3. Why is that so?

4. What if team members have differing discernment?

5. What is the best number of team members to be actively commanding the spirits to depart?

6. What should the lead minister do if he or she becomes weary?

7. If there are more than two team members, what should the rest of the team do while the lead members are ministering?

Biblical Foundations

8. What pattern was established for the deliverance ministry by Jesus?
   ➢ **Read Luke 10:1 & 17**

9. Did this pattern of teamwork continue in the early church in Acts? Name two examples.
   ➢ **Read Acts 18:18, Acts 15:40-41**

For Personal Reflection

10. When should the gender of the Deliverance Team be taken into account?

✺✺✺ Key Revelations to Ponder ✺✺✺

Who should lead the deliverance team? Frank had this to say:

Have you ever watched a wedge of geese in flight? The lead bird will buffet the wind for a few minutes and then he will drop back in the formation to "rest" while another moves into the lead position to take his place. The deliverance team can cooperate in similar fashion. The aim is to set the captive free and give the glory to Jesus, so it should make no difference who is leading the warfare.

THE DELIVERANCE TEAM
Answers to Chapter 17

1. From two to six ministers

2. Unity

3. Satan capitalizes on disunity.

4. Each should allow the other to address what they discern.

5. Usually one or two

6. Step back and allow another to take over.

7. Be in prayer, praise, and scripture reading.

8. Teams of two

9. a. A married team: Aquilla and Priscilla

   b. An apostolic team: Paul and Silas

10. (Personal reflection)

PRACTICAL SUGGESTIONS FOR THE DELIVERANCE MINISTER

*When evening came, they brought to Him many who were demon-possessed;
and He cast out the spirits with a word...*
−Matt. 8:16

How does one actually go about delivering a person from demon spirits? This is the practical side of deliverance. It is our purpose to share what has been gained by study, revelation, and experience. We urge, however, each person engaging in deliverance ministry to remain open to the Holy Spirit's teaching and guidance.

A pre-ministry interview or discussion is necessary to unlock the unique spiritual circumstances of the candidate. The purpose of the discussion is to detect the presence of spirits and uncover their nature. This is done through determining what are or have been problems in the life of the candidate. Current problems with the person usually have their roots in earlier life.

Prayer is especially appropriate at the time of deliverance. Any of those present may wish to lead in prayer. But before the actual deliverance gets underway the candidate should also pray. We often take a moment to allow the candidate to *transact* with Jesus, to give to Jesus anything that makes him or her feel unworthy or unlovely, and to reaffirm his or her love relationship with the Lord. This has tremendous effect on the spiritual atmosphere in the room and for the session.

It is not the loudness with which we speak that makes the demons tremble and obey, but the authority with which we speak in the name of Jesus. As Frank Hammond liked to jokingly point out: "Demons aren't deaf!"

Questions for Review

1. When preparing a suitable place for deliverance ministry, what practical considerations should be addressed?

2. What is the purpose of the pre-ministry conference?

3. Whether the session is "one on one" or a group meeting, why should notes be taken?

MINISTRY NOTES

It is important that these notes be kept secure to prevent anyone but the person receiving ministry and the deliverance team from seeing them. We often use a date and initials instead of names to avoid any future confidentiality concerns.

4. Following an opening prayer for guidance from the Holy Spirit, where is the natural place for the candidate to start during the pre-ministry conference?

5. Can demon activity still exist in a residual form after a Christian has found that their activity no longer seems to be a real problem?

6. What is often the root of current problems?

7. What should the deliverance minister do when a demon is detected?

8. List five things that hinder the deliverance.

9. How should the deliverance minister take authority over the evil spirits?

10. In what ways should the candidate cooperate?

11. What should the minister do if results are not immediate?

12. What is the blood of Jesus doing for the candidate?

Biblical Foundations

13. What do these scriptures tell you about the candidate's rescue and redemption?
    ➤ Read 1 Peter 1:18–19
    ➤ Read Col. 1:13–14

For Personal Reflection

14. What would be a good idea for the candidate to do prior to coming to the session?

15. Because of the atoning power of the blood of Jesus, what would best describe its effect against the powers of hell?

TIME BETWEEN MINISTRY SESSIONS

When bondages are broken during the deliverance session, the peace of God should settle on those in the room. However, there may still be further layers to uncover. Deliverance can at times be like peeling back the layers of an onion. We tell candidates to walk out their new found freedom for a period of 3 or 4 weeks. Then, they can reflect on the presence of the fruit of the Spirit in their life. If other issues have come to the surface, a follow-up session can be arranged.

Key Revelations to Ponder

Frank usually spoke to the demons in this manner: "Demons, I know that you are there. I know of your presence and of your evil works. I tell you that you have no right to stay in this person. This person belongs to Jesus Christ. Jesus purchased him with His own blood. This body is the temple of the Holy Spirit. Everything that defiles is cast out. You are a trespasser and you must go. I command you to go now in the name of Jesus."

When ministering deliverance, the blood of Jesus is packed with power. Some people do not understand "pleading the blood." It is not a matter of repeating the word "blood" over and over. Rather, give testimony of what the blood does for the believer. The blood redeems, cleanses, justifies and sanctifies the believer.

The blood of Jesus is *alive*! That is why demons hate it... it is still as powerful today as it was the moment that it flowed from His veins. The demons are defeated by the covering blood of Jesus.

– Frank Hammond

PRACTICAL SUGGESTIONS FOR THE DELIVERANCE MINISTER
Answers to Chapter 19

1. Privacy, seating, record-keeping materials, and supplies to handle vomiting, spitting or crying

2. To detect the presence of spirits and uncover their nature

3. There are a few reasons to take notes:

   1. To proceed in an orderly fashion.

   2. To provide the delivered individual with a record of the session thereby enabling him or her to resist the delivered spirits in the future.

   3. To provide a record for the team in case follow-up ministry is needed.

4. By recalling experiences and attitudes in early life that might have opened doors for demons to enter.

5. Yes — Demons can certainly be subdued by the power of the Holy Spirit within the person, but may remain there awaiting a weak moment in the person's life to regain control.

6. Experiences in early life

7. Look for companion demons

8. The five hindrances include:

   1. Unforgiveness

   2. Involvement in occult practice

   3. Abortion

   4. Unconfessed adultery

   5. Involvement in religious cults or false religions

9. The minister should:

   a. Bind the interfering of higher spirits.

   b. Bind the strong man, the ruling spirit.

   c. Command all indwelling spirits to unlink themselves from one another.

10. The candidate should:

    a. Refrain from praise, prayer, and speaking in tongues.

    b. Employ his or her own will against the demons.

    c. Address the spirits when told to do so by the minister.

    d. Begin to physically expel the spirit(s).

11. Be persistent

12. Cleansing, justifying and sanctifying the believer

13. He or she has been purchased back from Satan's power by the blood of Jesus.

14. To read a book on deliverance, and to prayerfully make a list of issues that he or she feel will need to be addressed. This saves a great deal of time!

15. It is the most powerful of weapons!

Pros & Cons on Techniques and Methods

*And this I pray, that your love may abound still more and more
in real knowledge and all discernment*
–Phil. 1:9

While it would be convenient to have pat formulas and prescribed methods of spiritual ministries, we must remain dependent upon the leading of the Spirit. In the case of the healing ministry and the deliverance ministry, it is often necessary to rely upon guidance and urging by the Holy Spirit as to how to proceed, when to shift focus, how to determine that the candidate is free, etc.

In addition, it is often special words from the Holy Spirit, provided through the gift of discernment, that unlock the door to liberation of the soul. One cannot regulate a gift of the Spirit. As Frank Hammond notes, if we start looking for methods and techniques and regulation, we will end up in hopeless confusion. That is exactly what the devil would like us to do!

Holy Spirit guidance is required for such issues as the laying on of hands, conversing with demons, the composition of the team, etc. when engaging in the ministry of deliverance.

Questions for Review

1. Can a deliverance minister employ the same techniques and methods for every deliverance session?

2. What should determine the techniques or methods used in ministry?

3. In what situations might the laying on of hands be inadvisable?

4. Some illnesses are rooted in demonic oppression. In these circumstances could the laying on of hands be a part of the process of deliverance?

AUTHORITY, NOT ROUTINE

The laying on of hands can be a trigger to faith in the candidate whether during a healing prayer or a deliverance prayer. If, however, we have complete confidence in our Christ-given authority, we can deliver people simply through our commands, in Jesus' Name.

5. What is a common tactic demons use to attempt to instill fear in the deliverance minister? What scriptures assure us that we need not fear?

6. What is to be gained by commanding a spirit to name itself?

7. What is the inherent danger in doing so?

8. What is the best physical position for the candidate to take?

Biblical Foundations

9. How does Frank Hammond interpret 1 Timothy 5:22?

10. Mark 16:17–18 calls for the laying on of hands for what purpose?

For Personal Reflection

11. Jesus was laying His hands on "all who were brought to Him." Do you think that this implies that deliverances were done with the laying on of hands?

    ➢ **Read Luke 4:40–41**

Key Revelations to Ponder

If we are willing to take the first step in ministering deliverance, the Holy Spirit will be there to guide how it will be accomplished.

Demons can indwell any part of the human body. One of the favorite areas seems to be the lower abdomen. When a hand is laid on this area in ministry the demons very often come up and out through the mouth more readily. This is why it is wise and helpful to have both men and women involved in the deliverance situation. Women can lay hands on the women and men on the men.

Frank Hammond liked to emphasize that the thing we must beware of is *fear of evil spirits*. The Bible gives us assurance that we can engage demon spirits in battle with absolutely no fear of them retaliating and harming us. Use common sense where necessary.

[Be] not in any way terrified by your adversaries, which is to them a proof of perdition [destruction], but to you of salvation, and that from God. Phil. 1:28

PROS AND CONS ON
TECHNIQUES & METHODS
Answers to Chapter 16

1.   No

2.   Each situation is different. The deliverance minister has to be sensitive to the leading of the Holy Spirit and the particular manifestations of the demons.

3.   If a spirit of lust or flirting was present; or if a "touch me not" spirit was manifesting.

4.   It would seem so.

5.   Threats of revenge against the minister are common. While common sense and Holy Spirit guidance help in this area, Luke 10:19 says that "nothing shall by any means hurt you," and Phil. 1:28 says "in nothing be terrified by your adversaries."

6.   Its power is more readily broken.

7.   It may lead to taking revelation from the wrong spiritual source.

8.   Sitting comfortably in a chair

9.   The prohibition of "laying on of hands" applies to ordination for leadership, not deliverance or healing ministry. However, a good practice is to never lay hands on someone prematurely.

10. Healing the sick

11. (Personal reflection)

MINISTRY to CHILDREN

"Permit the children to come to Me; do not hinder them;
for the kingdom of God belongs to such as these."
–Mark 10:14

It seems unfair and horrific that little children can be oppressed by demons. At the same time, it reveals the true nature of the enemy and the kind of warfare in which he is engaged.

Jesus Himself cast spirits out of children. In Luke 9, a man approaches Jesus begging for help because his son is sent into convulsions by a *spirit*. In Matthew 15, a woman approaches Jesus because her daughter is cruelly and grievously vexed by a *demon*. Frank notes that it is even possible for demonic spirits to affect an unborn child, due to inherited issues or the emotional state of the mother-to-be.

Ordinarily, children are quite easily delivered. Since the spirits have not been there very long they are not as deeply embedded in the flesh. There are exceptions to this, as in the cases of children who have been exposed to demonic attack through abuse. The manifestations in these cases can be quite dramatic, even in children.

There are four key differences between adult deliverance and the deliverance of a child. These are dealt with in detail in Frank Hammond's companion book *A Manual for Children's Deliverance*.

Questions for Review

1. When ministering deliverance to a child who is old enough to understand, how should he or she be prepared?

2. Who is the best person to hold the child during the deliverance prayer time?

THE LITTLE SKUNK

The Little Skunk is a children's book now available for the parent to read with the child, to explain deliverance in a way he or she can understand. Having this read prior to a deliverance session with a child is extremely beneficial.

3. How can a demon cause a child to react during deliverance prayer?

4. Who has the ultimate responsibility for serving as spiritual guardian(s) of the child?

5. In the case of Mary, what techniques did Ida Mae Hammond employ?

6. What would have happened if her father had stepped in and withdrawn his daughter from the deliverance session?

Biblical Foundations

7. Reread the account in Mark 7:24–30. Was the daughter present for the deliverance?

8. Does this account indicate that in cases where Godly parental authority exists children can be set free even if not present with a deliverance minister?

WHEN A CHILD IS NOT PRESENT...

In general, face-to-face ministry is preferable, but ministry without the child being present may occur when the child is too ill to transport, or when other hindrances might exist.

For Personal Reflection

9. How do you think these guidelines might differ when ministering to a teen instead of a child?

～～～ Key Revelations to Ponder ～～～

In these last days, children are exposed to far more demonic influence than ever before. It is vital for parents to take the lead in protecting their children as much as possible and to be alert to their child's behavior. The parent should be able to identify when the behavior has "gone over the line" from disobedience and normal fears, for instance, to a true deliverance need.

Frank and Ida Mae had a special affinity for ministering to children. They spoke frequently on the importance of the family and parental control.

Parents must take the initiative for their children. The parent must bring his child to Jesus. The father in Luke Chapter 9 brought his son, and the mother in Matthew 15 came to Jesus on behalf of her little daughter. The successful outcomes of these two ministries should encourage parents to seek deliverance for their children. In multiplied hundreds of cases, we have seen deliverance bring peace to the child and rest to the parents.

- Adapted from *A Manual for Children's Deliverance* by Frank Hammond

MINISTRY TO CHILDREN
Answers to Chapter 14

1. The child needs a simple explanation of what the minister will do, and to know that the minister is speaking to the "bad spirit" and not the child.

2. The parent(s)

3. The child can claim that they are being hurt or wronged and make a display by screaming, or crying. The child can try to get free of the one holding him or her and try to get a sympathetic parent to stop the session. This is quite common.

4. The parents are the spiritual guardians of the child.

5. Quietly commanding, gentle restraining, and responding to the demons as they identified themselves. As well, Ida Mae Hammond constantly reminded the child that she was addressing the demons, not Mary herself.

6. She would not have become free.

7. No

8. Yes

9. (Personal reflection)

The following books are valuable in helping parents in this role:

A Manual on Children's Deliverance by Frank Hammond

Deliverance for Children and Teens by Bill Banks

Kingdom Living for the Family by Frank Hammond

The Little Skunk by Sue Banks

INTERCESSORY PRAYER WARFARE

Christ Jesus is He who died, yes, rather who was raised,
who is at the right hand of God, who also intercedes for us.
–Rom. 8:34

Jesus taught us to intercede for one another that we might be delivered from the snares of the Devil. Indeed, Jesus Himself is interceding on our behalf right now, in heaven (Rom. 8:34).

For this reason, intercession touches the heart of the Lord. It is an act of love, to lay down one's life, even if temporarily, on behalf of another. Great good can come from such efforts, even though much of this kind of ministry takes place in the unseen, spiritual realm.

What can be done on behalf of others who are in obvious need of deliverance, but who are not open to receive it? A similar question can be asked; what can be done on behalf of others who are not saved, and who are not open to receive salvation?

Intercessory Prayer is a powerful tool in the hand of the believer. It can be a necessary tool for both saved and unsaved person alike. Too often Satan, the deceiver, is having his way in a person's life precisely because no one has interceded for him, and that person is held in needless bondage.

Questions for Review

1. What is the first point of consideration when dealing with intercessory prayer warfare?

2. What is the meaning of the Greek word for salvation (*soteria*)?

3. What, then, is the first stage of deliverance?

4. What should we pray to happen for those lost souls, blinded by Satan's power, for whom we are interceding?

5. What is the likely condition of the will of those who are not directly open to ministry, and for whom we are led to enter into spiritual warfare?

6. What word of a caution do the Hammonds offer regarding trying to control another's will?

7. Instead of praying to control the person's will (even if for a good purpose), for what do we pray?

8. What kind of atmosphere do we pray for in this kind of situation?

9. What should be the motivating force in our intercession?

10. What is a fruitful prayer technique in intercessory prayer?

Biblical Foundations

11. If there is someone for whom you are interceding to be set free, try substituting their name in the appropriate places in the scripture that follows. If helpful, write the passage below and insert their name into it.

> ➤ **Read Ephesians 1:17–21**

For Personal Reflection

12. Can you think of a scripture you can use to intercede for someone?

～～～ Key Revelations to Ponder ～～～

Anyone who will not accept the Lord's provision of salvation (or deliverance) is held by spiritual blindness. And whatever excuse is offered for rejecting salvation (or deliverance) represents some form of deception. Intercessory Prayer can be used to break through these demonic barriers.

Are you feeling called to intercede for cities and nations? Frank Hammond believed in the validity of this ministry: *"There are two levels of spiritual warfare. One level of warfare involves the casting out of demons. A second level of warfare is that of wrestling against principalities, powers and spirits of wickedness in the heavenlies. It is time for the Church to confront these spiritual Goliaths."*

Adapted from *The Saints at War* **by Frank Hammond**

 INTERCESSORY PRAYER
WARFARE
Answers to Chapter 13

1. The spiritual condition of the recipient of our prayer. Has he or she been born again?

2. Deliverance

3. Praying for the salvation of the one needing deliverance

4. That their spiritual blindness be removed

5. Their will may be so overridden by demonic forces that he or she is unable to respond to available help.

6. He recommends avoiding any prayer aimed at controlling another person's will. This would be considered witchcraft.

7. That their *will* be released from bondage in order to respond directly to the Lord and receive His help.

8. An atmosphere of change — that the person will first and foremost choose Christ and His Kingdom.

9. To love the real person as God loves them

10. Praying the scripture and inserting the name of the person into it

11. (Personal reflection)

12. (Personal reflection)

THE FINAL CONFLICT

Therefore, since we have so great a cloud of witnesses surrounding us,
let us also lay aside every encumbrance and the sin which so easily entangles us,
and let us run with endurance the race that is set before us...
–Heb. 12:1

In Chapter 23, Frank Hammond shares his dream and interpretation of the end-time battle being waged:

"The Lord told me that those in the stands were the great cloud of witnesses. They were all of the Christians who have ever lived and were now looking down upon the world from their heavenly position. All of the patriarchs and saints of the Old and New Testament eras were in the stands. They were the ones who had been in the 'pennant races' in former generations. Many of them had done well and were in the 'hall of fame' as recorded in Hebrews Chapter Eleven. They were looking with keenest of anticipation to see how those of us on the field in this generation would do.

Then the Lord said to me, 'THIS IS THE WORLD SERIES!'"

Questions for Review

1. In Chapter 23, Frank Hammond recounts a dream he had. It involved two opposing teams in an apparent baseball game. How did the Lord explain the significance of this game to Frank Hammond? Who were the two teams?

2. Do you think that the church of the first three centuries practiced deliverance? (Read the quotes taken from the early church fathers at the beginning of this Study Guide).

3. What areas of warfare are represented by the bases in Frank Hammond's dream?

4. What colors were the uniforms of the devil's team, and what was the significance of the two colors?

Biblical Foundations

5. Why is it vital to enter into this conflict with Satan and his demons?
   ➢ Read Revelation 12:11–12, 17

6. Signs will precede the return of Jesus, but will we know the exact time of His return?
   ➢ Read Matthew 24:36

7. We already know the outcome; who wins the battle?
   ➢ Review Revelation 12:11

For Personal Reflection

8. In the dream, God's people were playing defense. How can we get on the offense?

9. Does this dream and its interpretation encourage you?

Key Revelations to Ponder

It is obvious that along the way, the Church has lost a precious closeness to the Holy Spirit. According to JEROME, the Church "*lost as much of her power as it gained in wealth and secular power.*" However, the Holy Spirit has been restoring God's people through the centuries to their original anointing as experienced in the early Church. The anointing to cast out demons is one such ministry that is coming to the forefront, for an end-time, victorious Church!

THE FINAL CONFLICT
Answers to Chapter 23

1. "This is the World Series. This is the Final conflict between the forces of evil and the forces of righteousness. This is to determine the World Championship."

2. Yes!

3. Social, Business, Church, and Home

4. Black & White. These colors represent the mixture of truth and lies, and good and evil, that are characteristic of the enemy's ploys.

5. We are led to fight because of what Jesus has done for us, and due to the wrath of Satan who knows his time is short, and who has entered into war with the saints.

6. No

7. The Church; we do!

8. (Personal reflection)

9. (Personal reflection)

Did you enjoy studying *Pigs in the Parlor*?

Now get ready to dig deeper into the best-selling book *Breaking Unhealthy Soul Ties*. Learn the blessings of Godly Soul-Ties and how to break Ungodly Soul-Ties...

"Here at last is a thorough and theologically sound treatment of a little understood subject" - from the *Foreword* by Frank Hammond

Breaking Unhealthy Soul-Ties
by Bill & Sue Banks

Unhealthy soul-ties involve the control of one individual over another, and can be one of the most difficult blocks to spiritual freedom. Some relationships are healthy and bring blessings into our lives; other types of relationships can bring demonic bondage to our souls. This book assists the reader in diagnosing both healthy and unhealthy relationships, and offers positive steps to personal freedom.

STUDY GUIDE: Breaking Unhealthy Soul-Ties
by Bill & Sue Banks

This Study Guide is a tool that can be used to diagnose and address the soul-ties in your life.

This companion book provides detail into what the soul is, how it functions, and how it can be affected by both positive and negative ties.

EXCERPT FROM
THE BOOK:

BREAKING UNHEALTHY SOUL-TIES

BY BILL & SUE BANKS

AVAILABLE AT   www.impactchristianbooks.com

SOUL-TIES: GODLY AND UNGODLY

Perhaps it would be helpful at the outset to differentiate between godly soul-ties and ungodly soul-ties. Remember, a soul-tie is a bonding in the soulish realm; a bonding between the souls of two or more people. Although in today's thinking any links to another person are generally thought to be unhealthy, there are *healthy* and Godly soul-ties. The first soul-tie was designed by God and intended for the benefit of the first couple.

All soul-ties incorporate influence, compromise and obedience for the sake of peaceful coexistence. Godly soul-ties have a settling, peaceful influence and not only help to stabilize the relationship with another, but also with the Heavenly Father. I believe far more godly soul-ties exist than ungodly.

In an ungodly soul-tie, one individual pulls another away from his or her commitment to God's laws of morality and obedience. We think of such pulls as evil soul-ties, wherein the one who becomes linked with another person finds himself to be corrupted by the association. Paul warns against these types of relationships in 1 Corinthians:

Do not be deceived: "Bad company corrupts good morals."   1 Cor. 15:33 NASB

The literal meaning of this passage might be rendered, *do not let depraved companionship spoil or defile your moral habits* (i.e. your manner or acting).

Consider the godly soul-ties outlined in Scripture. God saw that man was incomplete alone. He was made for union. First and foremost, man was designed for union with Christ, for without God a void exists. Secondly, man was designed for union with his wife — his helpmate. Finally, man was designed for union with his fellow man.

Our first and primary soul-tie is therefore union with Christ. That is, be yoked with God.

> Take *my yoke* upon you, and learn of me; for I am meek and lowly in heart: and ye shall find rest unto your souls. Matt. 11:29

Christ calls His people into vital union with Him. In addition to the figure of the yoke, He also figuratively uses the connection of the branches to the vine as the means for the believers to draw sustenance and produce fruit.

We are called upon to be in vital union with Christ in a variety of metaphors and similes, such as being united with Him, the Bread from heaven, by which we are to sustain ourselves; as the Vine to which we are attached as branches; as the Head to which we are attached as members of His Body; as the Shepherd whose flock we are; a King and Lord whose subjects we are; and as the Bridegroom for whom we await as the Bride. We, as His Body, are called to be one; to exist in union with Him, and in unity with one another.

MAN AND THE CREATION

God wanted this world to be a visible representation of His invisible attributes, eternal power, and Divine nature.

All of God's creation is "very good" and was meant to give man provision and refreshment. Man, when he fully appreciates the beauty and intelligence of all things created as a representation of the beauty and intelligence of the Creator, will be able to form a healthy relationship with the world around him.

However, we are not to love the world, nor to become unduly attached to it; nor to things, even inanimate objects, so as to worship the creation rather than the Creator. There are curses attached to some objects. Soul-ties can be formed with objects through *sentimental attachment*; "I cannot part with it," "I can't live without it." Man can become so soul-bound to an animal that it takes precedence over human relationships. Attaching too much importance to things or to places allows such items to become idols for us.

> Love not the world, neither the things that are in the world. If any man love the world, the love of the Father is not in him.   1 John 2:15

The Greek word for love used in I John is *agapao,* to love with the God kind of love, in a social or moral sense. Man, however, has perverted the love of God and replaced it with the love of the world, His creation. Man has formed a soul-tie with the *created* instead of the *Creator.*

> I say that the things which the Gentiles sacrifice, they sacrifice to demons and not to God; and I do not want you to become **sharers in demons.**   1 Cor. 10:20 NASB

> Professing themselves to be wise, they became fools, And changed the glory of the uncorruptible God into an image made like to corruptible man, and to birds, and fourfooted beasts, and creeping things ... Who changed the truth of God into a lie, and **worshipped and served the creature more than the Creator,** who is blessed for ever. Amen. Rom. 1:22–25

This attachment opens the way for demonic invasion of a person's life. Matthew states that one cannot serve two masters (Matt. 6:24). To be linked to Christ means to view His creation as a revelation *of* the Creator.

It is possible for man to bind himself to demons by turning a created thing into an object of worship or by seeking protection from it, as in witchcraft. But for the purposes of this book we will limit ourselves primarily to those soul-ties which occur between two or more human beings and the potential for bondages to develop in those relationships.

UNION WITH SPOUSE AND FAMILY

In the marriage union, husband and wife become one flesh as seen in God's command to Adam and Eve:

> Therefore shall a man leave his father and his mother, and **shall cleave unto his wife:** and they shall be one flesh.   Gen. 2:24

The first soul-tie was designed and intended for the first couple. In the first command or principle given to man regarding marriage, God required the man entering marriage to "leave" and "cleave." That is, he should break the emotional soul-ties and the control of his parents, replacing them with a godly soul-tie by cleaving to his wife. God speaks of making of two individuals into one new flesh, or one single individual. The visible memorial of this union is the child with which the union is blessed.

Because man's deepest emotions involve his feelings toward his mate, or potential mate, this is a primary area for soul-tie danger. Man has mistakenly relegated marriage to an agreement between two people, rather than a lifelong, God-ordained, covenant tie. Thus like many other arrangements between people, it has, in at least fifty-percent of the cases, become doomed to failure.

EVEN GOD-ORDAINED, COVENANT SOUL-TIES CAN BE BROKEN

Ungodly soul-ties can lead to the dissolution of marriage. A very common type of soul-tie which is involved in the breakup of marriages is that formed with another woman outside the marriage. Such soul-ties may be formed as the result of a physical, sexual union (as in I Cor. 6:16), or because of an emotional soul-tie which may or may not consciously start out with any type of dating or sexual overtones. These are often simply friendships which become something more.

The other woman initially either fills some sort of void, that of a mother figure, friend, companion, or workplace partner, or offers an easy escape from the necessary responsibilities and effort required to maintain a healthy marriage. In recent decades these problems have increased astronomically due to the epidemic of divorce and have placed so many divorced people (especially women) in the work place. Lonely people seek someone to alleviate their loneliness, and working together creates opportunities for many snares to be laid. Today there are many women who want to find a man at any cost, and many men devoid of moral standards.

The inability to break with *preexisting* ungodly soul-ties can also contribute to the breakup of marriages. The young man who cannot break free from "his mother's apron strings," as it is usually expressed, is a poor candidate for a strong or successful marriage. Some overcome this type of pressure by moving away which is usually a great help. I have counseled with several women whose husbands seemed to be unable to make any decisions without first consulting mother. Several have complained that his mother would demand (or expect) him to be at her house to take care of her needs and of her house, while the wife and children were neglected, and their own house fell into a state of disrepair.

The new husband who seems unable to grow up and face his responsibilities, and cannot break the soul-ties with his former evil or immature companions, is also a poor candidate for marriage. These men feel they have to go out every night with their male friends to bars, strip joints or other entertainment, and then cannot understand why they can't quit drinking, smoking or doing drugs, as they have promised themselves and their wives.

A successful young businessman of about twenty-eight came and received salvation and the Baptism in the Holy Spirit in our prayer room; later he came back for deliverance. He confessed that he was having a problem breaking free from smoking pot. He had a history of drug use during his previous career as a professional athlete but wanted to be completely clean for his marriage and to be able to honorably follow the Lord. He admitted that a part of his problem in staying free was that his best friend, another very successful businessman, was still actively smoking pot and offered him some every time they were together. He usually met his friend at least one night a week. He and his wife were praying for his victory, but he kept failing due to the pressure from his friends. This illustrates the truth of the Scripture previously mentioned:

> ...evil communications [associations, fellowship] corrupt good manners [good conduct, good intentions].   1 Cor. 15:33b [BRACKETS OURS]

Forgiveness and kindness strengthen the healthy marriage bond between two people. Furthermore, as Ecclesiastes points out, *a threefold cord is not quickly broken* (4:12). God hates divorce, and certainly a shared, active faith in Christ will knit the two partners firmly together, causing their house to remain standing even after storms have come.

CULTIC SOUL-TIES

Soul-ties normally exist within cultic organizations. A linking of the people occurs through mind-control usually in mutual allegiance to a cultic leader or to cultic beliefs and doctrines, such as white supremacy, or satanic beliefs.

Unfortunately, as we have previously demonstrated, some soul-ties are ungodly, unnatural and evil. A negative soul-tie is subtle, and like a cancer, grows slowly, undetected. If you never look in a mirror, you won't discover the smudge of dirt on your face. The perfect law of liberty is the Word of God, the mirror to discover flaws that need correcting.

Satan, through a spirit of anti-Christ, has always fervently sought to draw man's soul after himself, and he uses self-centered individuals, cults and gurus, and the occult. Man can literally sell his soul through a conscious pledge of allegiance to a satanic religion or its representatives. The fact that man may not fully believe in Satan's reality and power does not prevent him from bonding his soul to the devil, through ungodly spiritual activity. There is no gray area of non-commitment. Man was created to be in relationship with the invisible, the spiritual, and has to make a conscious decision to unite his soul to Christ. That is the ultimate good soul-tie and by any standard the greatest one of all.

Witchcraft

An evil soul-tie is actually a form of witchcraft. Witchcraft is spiritual. It is essentially defined as one person's control over another person.

> **Witchcraft** – the manipulation, control, or domination of one person by another person. Unhealthy soul ties between individuals are often a form of witchcraft, to varying degrees.

For example, if I were exercising witchcraft on you, I would be attempting to get you to do my will by a power that is not the Holy Spirit. The power involved is, in the best light, a form of psychic or soulish power, and is at worst satanic or demonic. Satan is the author of bondages and loves to see people restricted, tormented, helpless or hopeless. This is the subtle form of witchcraft or control practiced by one person over another.

1. Conscious Witchcraft

Overt witchcraft involves conscious awareness of what is being done. The source of the power is not of God but comes through an occult practitioner. The one practicing it is either himself a witch/warlock, or has employed the assistance of an actual practitioner of witchcraft to place the spell, or curse, upon the other party. There is no such thing as "white witchcraft," there is only witchcraft.

In conjuring up such spells the practitioner may use personal items, such as hair or articles of clothing to work the spell. The spells have various effects: the individual may be unable to sleep, find himself tormented, unable to have financial success (losing jobs, etc.), unable to make friends, estranged from old friends, or unable to find any peace unless he returns to the person he or she has left. Such spells may have such wording as: "Bring Joe back to me; don't ever let him be happy with anyone else! Don't let him have any satisfaction until he returns. Make him come back! Give him trouble until he marries me!"

One of the most common characteristics of witchcraft is its emasculation of males. Witchcraft is traditionally matriarchal. The women wear the pants; the role of the man is either abdicated or usurped, resulting in his emasculation.

2. UNCONSCIOUS WITCHCRAFT

The person who simply "prays amiss" may be making the very same pronouncements, but is unaware that he or she is practicing unconscious witchcraft, and unaware that the power of Satan is being utilized. The person may not even believe in Satan or in witchcraft. However, the power is still the same.

A prayer uttered because of a need for revenge or control can create a source of harassment against the other person. If a soul-tie has existed between the two, this unconscious form of control or witchcraft practiced by one will continue to oppress the other.

Every prayer is heard, but the question is by whom? God does not honor prayers of revenge or manipulation — but we firmly believe Satan does. A believer praying in the wrong spirit can harm the other with subtle oppression. It is extremely important that we guard our prayers by praying according to the will of God. God has made it abundantly clear that we are allowed to pour out our complaints before Him, but we must divest ourselves of unforgiveness, resentment, and bitterness.

SUMMARY

We tend to be the most vulnerable to those closest to us. We are rarely subject even to the subtle domination of a stranger. The key to avoiding such bondages is to know the truth about soul-ties and thus to be forewarned, and forearmed, to be able to willfully resist them.

DVD VIDEOS

DVD TEACHING SERIES
by Frank Hammond

Frank Hammond amplifies and expands the teachings from *Pigs in the Parlor* in a series of Video DVDs. In these DVDs, he reveals additional truths gleaned from his far-reaching ministry in the area of deliverance and related fields. In particular, Frank teaches and ministers for 3 hours on the Schizophrenia hands diagram from *Pigs in the Parlor* on the DVD entitled "The Schizophrenia Revelation."

Watch excerpts now at:
www.impactchristianbooks.com/revelation

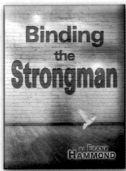

* All DVDs are U.S.A. Standard - NTSC Encoded

Books & Ebooks on Children's Deliverance

ISBN 0892280786

A MANUAL FOR CHILDREN'S DELIVERANCE
BY FRANK HAMMOND

A book to help parents minister to children, and a valuable tool for parents to learn how to set their children free from spiritual bondages. Learn the basics of how to effectively minister to children. Topics include: Jesus' ministry to children, When the womb is unsafe, Methods for ministering to children, Occult Infiltration, A child's imagination, and more.

DELIVERANCE FOR CHILDREN & TEENS
BY BILL BANKS

A practical handbook for ministering deliverance to children. The material in this book is arranged to help parents diagnose their children's problems and find solutions for destructive behavior. Includes a discussion of generational or hereditary issues, the role of discipline in the home, ministering to adopted children, and help for teens.

ISBN 0892280344

THE LITTLE SKUNK
BY SUSAN BANKS

A children's story book! For the child to read with a parent to understand the subject of deliverance without fear. Includes color illustrations to accompany the story, and assistance at the end for the parent to pray with the child. Watch how Charlie, Billy and Susie try to get the little skunk out of their house! (Deliverance need not be frightening if properly presented).

ISBN 0892281200

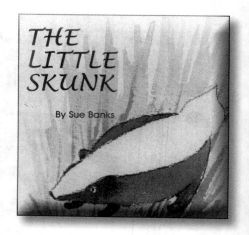

Other Frank Hammond Books & Ebooks

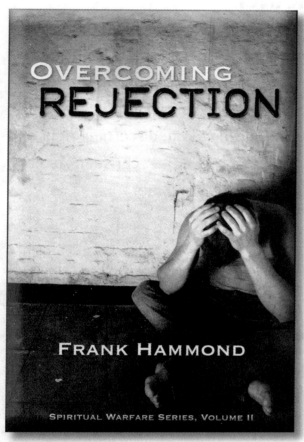

ISBN 0892281057

OVERCOMING REJECTION

Frank Hammond addresses the all-too-common root problem of rejection and the fear of rejection in the lives of believers, and provides steps to be set free. Learn how past experiences can influence our actions, and how we can be made whole.

Discover the various causes of rejection, including abuse, peer rejection, marital rejection, Church related rejection, and others. Learn about the remedy for rejection, and find prayers you can pray to be delivered!

THE BREAKING OF CURSES

The Bible refers to curses over 230 times, and 70 sins that cause curses are put forth in Scripture. Learn how Curses are just as real today as in Biblical times. This book shows what curses are and how you may deliver yourself and your family from them.

Learn more about Generational Curses, Personal Curses, Accursed Things, Word Curses, Authority Curses, Witchcraft Curses, Laws Governing Curses, and most importantly, Steps To Breaking Curses.

ISBN 089228109X

Other Frank Hammond Books & Ebooks

DEMONS & DELIVERANCE
IN THE MINISTRY OF JESUS

As a sequel to Pigs in the Parlor, this book sets forth guiding principles from Scripture and the ministry of Jesus for confronting demons and delivering the oppressed. You will learn about the nature and function of the demonic kingdom; discerning right and wrong methods of deliverance; fears that defeat christian soldiers; the believer's commission and authority; and more.

ISBN 0892280018

THE SAINTS AT WAR

Spiritual warfare over families, churches, cities and nations... Frank Hammond presents a study in warfare in the heavenlies, and explains how to pray for cities and nations. Learn how each Christian is equipped as a soldier, and how Christians can change lives, families, communities and nations, and more!

ISBN 0892281049

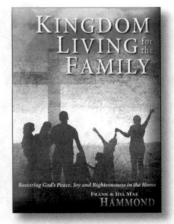

KINGDOM LIVING
FOR THE FAMILY

Families today are hurting and broken as never before. Many are frustrated by the cycle of strife and discord between husbands and wives, and between parents and children. In this book, Frank and Ida Mae Hammond reveal God's strong desire to heal and deliver the family, and they present a realistic plan to bring its members into a place of security within God's will.

ISBN 0892281006

COMFORT FOR THE WOUNDED SPIRIT

Help and comfort for the hurting Christian. This book is a message of hope and healing for those who are 'downtrodden, bruised, crushed and broken by calamity' (Lk. 4:18). The Hammonds show how deliverance from unclean spirits and the healing of inner wounds are separate yet companion ministries.

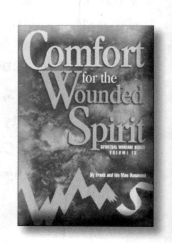

ISBN 0892280778

The Deliverance Audio Series...

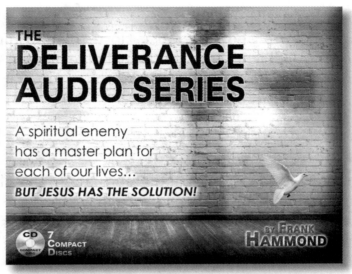

Listen to an excerpt now at:

www.impactchristianbooks.com/deliverance

THE DELIVERANCE SERIES (ON COMPACT DISC)

BY FRANK HAMMOND

In this companion teaching to *Pigs in the Parlor*, Frank Hammond covers the basics of deliverance and includes an in-depth discussion of the Schizophrenia Hands Diagram and the groupings of demonic spirits. Also included is an explanation of the root spirits of Rejection and Rebellion, how to maintain deliverance, and how to distinguish between impulses of the flesh and impulses of demonic spirits.

The CDs included in this series are:

- Healing the Personality
- The Schizophrenia Revelation, (I & II)
- Maintaining Deliverance
- Dealing with Pressures
- Demonic Doorways
- Group Ministry

OTHER COMPACT DISC SERIES BY FRANK HAMMOND INCLUDE:

FREEDOM FROM BONDAGE SERIES

FAMILY IN THE KINGDOM SERIES

THE FAITH SERIES

THE CHURCH SERIES

MESSAGE ON LOVE

END-TIME SERIES

SPIRITUAL MEAT SERIES

RECOGNIZING GOD SERIES

WALK IN THE SPIRIT SERIES

Frank Hammond Booklets & Ebooks

CONFRONTING FAMILIAR SPIRITS
0892280174

A person can form and develop a close relationship with an evil spirit, willfully or through ignorance, for knowledge or gain. When a person forms a relationship with an evil spirit, he then has a familiar spirit. Familiar spirits are counterfeits of the Holy Spirit's work.

REPERCUSSIONS FROM SEXUAL SINS
0892282053

The sexual revolution has impacted our nation, our church and our family. Promiscuity, nudity and sexual obscenities have become commonplace. The inevitable consequence of defilement is the loss of fellowship with a holy God. Learn how to break free from the bondage of sexual sin.

THE MARRIAGE BED
0892281863

Can the marriage bed be defiled? Or, does anything and everything go so long as husband and wife are in agreement with their sexual activities? Drawing from God's emphasis on purity and holiness in our lives, this booklet explains how to avoid perverse sexual demonic activity in a home.

SOUL TIES
0892280166

Good soul ties covered include marriage, friendship, parent/child, between christians. Bad soul ties include those formed from fornication, evil companions, perverted family ties, with the dead, and demonic ties through the church. Learn how you can be set free from demonic soul ties.

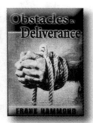

OBSTACLES TO DELIVERANCE: WHY DELIVERANCE SOMETIMES FAILS
0892282037

Why does deliverance sometimes fail? This is, in essence, the same question raised by Jesus' first disciples, when they were unable to cast out a spirit of epilepsy. Jesus gave a multi-part answer which leads us to take into account the strength of the spirit confronted and the strategy of warfare employed.

THE PERILS OF PASSIVITY
089228160X

Some have made deliverance their ultimate goal in life. Deliverance is not a final goal, it is only a sub-goal on the way to fulfill God's purpose in life. God said to Pharaoh, "Let my people go that they may serve Me..." (Exod. 7:16). There is a purpose in God for each of us - and it is not passivity! Passivity is a foe — it will even block deliverance.

Frank Hammond Booklets & Ebooks

PROMOTED BY GOD
089228093X

Ever wonder how Frank Hammond received his powerful anointing to minister healing and deliverance for the Lord? Find out in this personal testimony. Also, find answers to the questions: Is the Baptism in the Holy Spirit for today?, What was the purpose of this baptism? What were the qualifications for it? Were tongues a part of this experience? Did tongues have any useful purpose?"

OUR WARFARE
0892280921

On Christians in conflict with territorial spirits. In 2 Cor. 10, we are alerted that there is a war. Our war is a spiritual war. Our Commander in Chief has issued us the required weaponry and has given His name as our authority. Let us take up our warfare and defeat the enemy!

THE STRONGMAN OF UNBELIEF
0892280956

God raises this question: *"Who has believed our report? And to whom has the arm of the Lord been revealed?" Isa. 53:1.* What is the full report? Isaiah 53 tells us it is the full gospel, all that Jesus appropriated for us on the Cross. It is salvation from sin unto eternal life, but it is much so more than that! The Devil's goal is to torment and defeat us by keeping us in unbelief.

TALES OF TWO FRANKS
0892280662

From the lives of Frank Hammond and Frank Marzullo, come 40 miraculous deliverance testimonies! In this booklet, they tell some of their most memorable experiences. You will be encouraged as they readily admit the mistakes and failures they experienced, along with the amazing victories and unexpected spiritual happenings.

THE FATHER'S BLESSING
0892280743

The body of Christ is missing out on something of great significance - The Father's Blessing. Through surveys in multiple conferences, Frank Hammond has found that very few persons have ever received a father's blessing through their earthly fathers. Learn how you too can be blessed!

Miraculous Testimonies of
DELIVERANCE

089228031X

POWER FOR DELIVERANCE - THE SONGS OF DELIVERANCE
BY BILL BANKS

This **book,** and also **e-book,** shows that there is help for oppressed, tormented, and compulsive people, and that the solution is as old as the ministry of Jesus Christ. From over 30 years of counseling and ministering deliverance, in the United States and abroad, Bill Banks highlights the common root causes of emotional and mental torment, and walks the reader through steps to be set free. Read numerous case studies of people who have been delivered from their torments and fears, including testimonies of over 60 spirits...

Drugs	**Anger**	**Cancer**	**Pornography**	**Perversion**
Fears	**Harlotry**	**Hatred**	**Witchcraft**	**Rebellion**
Cocaine	**Rejection**	**Temper**	**Occult Spirits**	**Childlessness**
Terror	**Torment**	**Suicide**	**Disobedience**	**Unforgiveness**
Smoking	**Murder**	**Bitterness**	**Homosexuality**	**Foolishness**
Sleeping Disorder		**Abuse of Women**	**& more!**	

Other Frank Hammond Books & Ebooks

9780892283682

THE DISCERNING OF SPIRITS

We are equipped by God for spiritual warfare through the gifts of the Holy Spirit mentioned in 1 Corinthians 12. God has said that these are the channels through which His power will flow, the avenues through which His Holy Spirit will operate. Chief among these gifts for the ministry of deliverance is the gift of the *discerning of spirits.* Frank Hammond explains the application of this gift to the believer, and provides examples of how it has worked in his own ministry.

PRAISE: A WEAPON OF WARFARE & DELIVERANCE

Praise is a powerful weapon in deliverance and spiritual warfare. As you praise the Lord, things begin to happen in the unseen realm. When Saul was troubled by an evil spirit, the only thing they knew to help him was to call David. When David began to play on his harp and sing praise to his God, the evil spirit departed from King Saul. A demon cannot exist in that atmosphere — he simply cannot function.

9780892283859

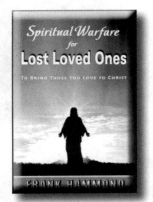

9780892283842

SPIRITUAL WARFARE FOR LOST LOVED ONES

Through spiritual warfare, intercessory prayer, and the ministry of love, we are able to help create the best possible environment around a loved one to come to know Jesus. But we must not lose our closeness with the Lord in the process, as these situations can be quite challenging to our spiritual walk. Frank Hammond says, "Don't let your family or friends go without resistance. Get in the spiritual battle, fight for your loves ones!"

POLTERGEISTS - DEMONS IN THE HOME

Do you, or someone you know, have demonic spirits in the home? Are you thrust out of sleep by banging doors, the sound of footsteps, lights going on and off? Do you see mysterious shadows on the wall or creatures at the foot of your bed? If so, there is good news for you. Your house can be cleansed! Just as the inside man can be swept clean of demonic spirits, so too can a house or a dwelling be swept clean from the evil presence and harassment of demonic spirits.

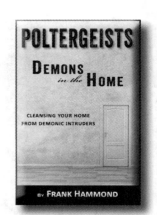

9780892283903

Books & E-books
On Healing & Baptism in the Holy Spirit

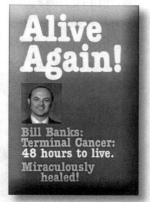

0892280484

ALIVE AGAIN

One of the greatest healing testimonies in print. A healing from cancer lasting over 30 years! And a powerful explanation of the baptism of the Holy Spirit, including prayers to receive this special touch from the Lord.

With six different terminal conditions, and numerous malignant tumors, read how one man sought the healing accounts in Scripture for strength and encouragement. Follow his story as he fights to live during 6 months of chemotherapy, radiation, and dialysis, and then is told he has only 48 hours to live! When the doctors gave up — God didn't. (**Book or Ebook**)

OVERCOMING BLOCKS TO HEALING

From 30 years of ministering in hospitals, churches, and homes, Bill Banks explains why some people are not healed, and what they can do about it.

0892281367

Has Jesus changed His mind, or are there blocks to healing as a part of Satan's strategy to keep us sick? Find answers to over 30 questions about God's willingness to heal, including divine revelations about Paul's Thorn, Job's battle with sickness, and the Scriptural distinction between instantaneous miracles and gradual healings. Included are testimonies of people healed from deafness, cancer, blindness, bad backs, crippled legs and arms, and more. (**Book or Ebook**)

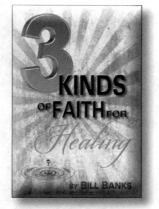

0892281030

THREE KINDS OF FAITH FOR HEALING

Many today have been taught that we must somehow "work up" or develop enough personal faith in order to be healed, and then we will experience God's move on our body. There is good news, however, because that teaching is simply not true! Jesus, for instance, ministered to the problem of blindness in at least five different ways on various occasions. He was, and is today, creative in His methods. He knows exactly how to minister to the needs of individuals at the level of their spiritual as well as their physical need. (**Book or Ebook**)

Deliverance from Emotional, Physical & Eating Disorders

0892280328

DELIVERANCE FROM FAT & EATING DISORDERS

Powerful help for those who have been unable to lose weight, and for those struggling with anorexia and bulimia. Learn about unnatural weight gain (or loss), and common spiritual roots.

Most people really have no idea as to why they overeat, and often live in continual condemnation for not having sufficient will-power to stop. Many have experienced rejection or feel that they are unattractive. There is a solution to obesity, and it is as old as the ministry of Jesus Christ. Included are fifteen Testimonies of people who found freedom from the bondage of excess weight! And find prayers for deliverance from fat. **(Book or Ebook)**

MINISTERING TO ABORTION'S AFTERMATH

Have you had an abortion? Do you carry guilt or fear inside due to this experience? Could miscarriage or infertility be rooted in past abortions? Does Jesus yearn to deliver all who are in bondage? Are you free to be all that God intended you to be?

0892280573

Abortion is a doorway to demonic attack. Many women were unaware of the physical, emotional and spiritual consequences, and still carry the trauma of the event with them - even in later years. Read a dozen real-life stories of women who have found deliverance and freedom from the various bondages associated with abortion, including emotional torment, physical complications, and more. Learn how their triumph can be yours. **(Book or Ebook)**

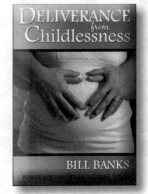

0892281030

DELIVERANCE FROM CHILDLESSNESS

Are you aware that demonic spirits can prevent childbirth? Or, that the Bible has a lot to say about childlessness? This book contains a wealth of information on ministry and healing to childless couples, and ministers to women and men with truths to overcome barrenness. Find the first real hope for certain childless couples, because for some, there can be a spiritual block preventing conception. **(Book or Ebook)**

Keys to Unlock
Bible Prophecy

0892280980

THE THIRD TOWER OF BABEL
by Stephen Banks

The most exalted image of Jesus Christ, the symbol of His Second Coming, has been overlooked during centuries of biblical research. Now, from the pages of Zechariah, Isaiah, and Daniel, this remarkable symbol of the Messiah is revealed.

Through this symbol of Jesus Christ you will find the key to unlock a 5000 year mystery involving the Ark of the Covenant, the coming New World Order, and the Second Coming of Jesus Christ.

MIRACLES
IN THE PETÉN

by Nancy Henson

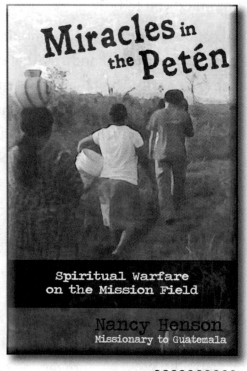

0892282002

SPIRITUAL WARFARE ON THE GUATEMALAN MISSION FIELD

Nancy Henson has seen many miracles in the villages of the Petén in northern Guatemala. Through her work as a medical missionary, she has witnessed miraculous healings, divine intervention, even someone close to her being raised from the dead.

Because of her efforts to bring the light of Jesus to this ancient region of Mayandom, she has also come up against Satanic powers and principalities in the spiritual realm. She has waged war against them in her quest to reclaim the heart of the Mayan for Jesus Christ.

Is God Trying to Speak to you?

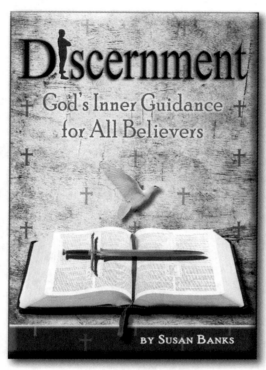

9780892282302

DISCERNMENT - GOD'S INNER VOICE FOR ALL BELIEVERS
BY SUSAN BANKS
(PAPERBACK OR E-BOOK)

Most Christians do not understand the necessity in discerning a situation or message. Without discernment, many in the Body of Christ are being led astray.

There are four basic steps you can follow to discern any message or messenger: Means, Motive, Morals and the Message. Using these four steps, you can know in your heart whether God is speaking to you or not. Ultimately, properly implemented discernment will bear good fruit for you, your family, and the Kingdom of God.

A deeper relationship with the Holy Spirit is needed for the times to come, including especially His gift of discernment.

NOTES

Impact Christian Books

These books are available through your local bookstore,
or you may order directly from
Impact Christian Books.

Website: www.impactchristianbooks.com

Phone Order Line: **(314)-822-3309**

Address: Impact Christian Books
332 Leffingwell Ave. Suite #101
Kirkwood, MO 63122